Parcel and Small Package Delivery Industry

Parcel and Small Package Delivery Industry

WILLIAM T. DENNIS

Copyright © 2011 by William T. Dennis

All rights reserved. No parts of this book may be reproduced, stored in a retrieval system, or transmitted in any form or by any means without permission in writing from the author.

ISBN 13: 9781461021544
ISBN 10: 1461021545
Library of Congress Control Number: 2011904791
CreateSpace, North Charleston, SC

Disclaimer:
Material presented is with the understanding the writer is not rendering legal or professional service. Users of this material are responsible to make sure the information contained within this book is applicable to their situation. When legal or other services are needed, retain the appropriate professionals.

ABOUT THE AUTHOR

WILLIAM T. DENNIS has over forty years of knowledge and experience in the fields of electronic engineering technology, freight transportation management, and third-party logistics management. His work history includes over twenty-five years with a major rail carrier, where he supervised and managed railroad yard operations in the Baltimore terminal and railroad traffic control installation projects in Huntington, West Virginia. He is currently with a nationally recognized logistics industry leader, headquartered in New Freedom, PA. William holds a B.S. from Capitol College and an M.B.A. from Marshall University.

AUTHOR'S NOTE

INFORMATION PRESENTED is readily available from many Internet sources and government publications. It was the writer's intent to organize information for easy reference. Information of this type can become dated; therefore, it is important to always verify reference material to insure it is current.

CONTENTS

Introduction XIII

SECTION I – PARCEL DELIVERY ENVIRONMENT 1

1.0 Importance of Parcel Delivery Service 4
1.1 Role of Parcel Carriers 4
    1.1.1 Cargo Transported 5
    1.1.2 Impact on Retailing 6
1.2 Typical Carrier System 6
    1.2.1 Financial Comparison 7
    1.2.2 Operating Comparisons 7
    1.2.3 Workforce Characteristics 8
    1.2.4 Variable verses Fixed Networks 8
    1.2.5 Integrated Networks 8
    1.2.6 Joint-Line verses Single-Line Service 9
1.3 Dominant Carriers 9
    1.3.1 United Parcel Service (UPS) 9
    1.3.2 FedEx Corporation (FedEx) 10
    1.3.3 United States Postal Service (USPS) 12
1.4 Delivery Options 14
    1.4.1 Domestic Service Offerings 14
    1.4.2 International Delivery Services 16
1.5 Parcel Classification 17
1.6 Types of Loads 18
1.7 Shipping Hazards 18
1.8 Industry's Competitive Structure 20
    1.8.1 Origin and Destination 20
    1.8.2 Consumer Requirements 21
    1.8.3 Delivery Speed 21
    1.8.4 Shape and Weight 22
1.9 LTL Sector 23
1.10 Parcel Consolidators 24
    1.10.1 Parcel Select Rates 24
    1.10.2 Brief History 24
    1.10.3 Consolidators versus Expeditors 25
1.11 Electronic Commerce (E-commerce) 26
    1.11.1 Differentiating B2B and B2C 26
    1.11.2 E-commerce Advantages and Drawbacks 26
    1.11.3 Market Share and Predicted Growth 27

1.12	**Dynamics of Home Delivery**	**28**
	1.12.1 Impact on Delivery Carriers	29
	1.12.2 Carriers Home Delivery Offerings	31
	1.12.3 Home Delivery Issues	31
1.13	**Wireless Information Technology**	**32**
	1.13.1 Bar Code	33
	1.13.2 Radio Frequency Identification (RFID)	34
	1.13.3 Mobile Printers	35
	1.13.4 Mobile Handheld Computers	36
1.14	**Sortation Systems Technologies**	**37**
1.15	**Global Environment**	**38**
	1.15.1 Global Shipping Complexities	39
	1.15.2 Global Airfreight Service	40
	1.15.3 Navigating the Global Marketplace	40

SECTION II – GENERAL PACKAGING GUIDELINES 43

2.0	**Container (or Package) Types**	**45**
2.1	**Load Types**	**46**
2.2	**Package Acceptability**	**47**
	2.2.1 Stationary	47
	2.2.2 Liquids	47
	2.2.3 Aerosols	48
2.3	**Elements of Packaging**	**48**
	2.3.1 Exterior Packaging	48
	2.3.2 Cushioning	49
	2.3.3 Closure, Sealing, and Reinforcing	51
	2.3.4 Marking and Labeling	55
2.4	**Protecting Perishables**	**57**
	2.4.1 Insulation	57
	2.4.2 Refrigerants	58
	2.4.3 Protective Packaging	61
2.5	**Hazardous Materials**	**62**
	2.5.1 Hazardous Material Regulations	62
	2.5.2 Classification	63
	2.5.3 Material Designation and Communication	64
	2.5.4 Performance Oriented Packaging (POP)	67
	2.5.5 Stench Packaging	69
	2.5.6 DOT Exemption Packaging	70
2.6	**Export Packaging**	**71**
	2.6.1 Packaging Standards	71
	2.6.2 Packaging Process	72
	2.6.3 Marking and Labeling	73

2.6.4 Unitization	74
2.6.5 Pallets	75

2.7 Shipping Containers 75
2.8 Corrugated Boxes 76
    2.8.1 Types of Corrugated Boxes 77
    2.8.2 Box Dimensions 79
    2.8.3 Box Performance 80
    2.8.4 Box Manufacturer's Certificate (BMC) 81
2.9 Other Shipping Containers 83
    2.9.1 Drums and Cans 83
    2.9.2 Barrels 83
    2.9.3 Steel Pails 84
    2.9.4 Sacks 84
    2.9.5 Bags 85
    2.9.6 Tubes 85
2.10 ESD-Protective Packaging 86
2.11 Pre-shipment Container Testing 87
    2.11.1 ASTM D 4169 87
    2.11.2 ISTA Pre-shipment Test Procedure 88
    2.11.3 ISTA 3A, 2004 Test 89
2.12 Vendor Packaging Compliance 90

SECTION III – MANAGING PARCEL SHIPMENTS 91

3.0 Basic Considerations 93
3.1 Parcel Pricing Components 94
    3.1.1 Published and Negotiated Rates 94
    3.1.2 Delivery Options 95
    3.1.3 Weight and Zone Pricing 95
    3.1.4 Parcel Characteristics 96
    3.1.5 Accessorial Charges 97
    3.1.6 Fuel Surcharge 97
    3.1.7 Service Charges 97
3.2 Multicarrier Shipping Solutions 98
    3.2.1 Internet-based Solutions 98
    3.2.2 Solution Features 99
3.3 Selecting a Carrier 100
    3.3.1 Parcel Delivery Alternatives 100
    3.3.2 Critical Elements 101
3.4 Freight Audit and Payment 103
    3.4.1 Types of Audit and Payment Firms 103
    3.4.2 Issues and Concerns 104
    3.4.3 Outsourcing 105

	3.4.4 Selecting a Provider	106
	3.4.5 Automating the Process	107
3.5	**Accessorial Charges**	**108**
	3.5.1 Purpose	108
	3.5.2 Monitor and Control	109
3.6	**Size and Weight Restrictions**	**109**
	3.6.1 Oversize Parcels	111
	3.6.2 Dimensional Weight	111
	3.6.3 Size Matters	112
3.7	**Shipment Consolidation**	**113**
3.8	**Loss, Damage, and Delay Claims**	**114**
	3.8.1 Types of Damage	115
	3.8.2 Responsibilities	115
	3.8.3 Filing Loss and Damage Claims	117
	3.8.4 Overcharge Claim	117
	3.8.5 Suit Deadline	118
3.9	**Contracting**	**119**
	3.9.1 Historical Overview	120
	3.9.2 Shipper's Profile	121
	3.9.3 What Contracting Method?	122
	3.9.4 Sourcing	123
	3.9.5 Notification	124
	3.9.6 Evaluation and Award	125
	3.9.7 Contract Administration	126

SECTION IV – APPENDICES **127**

#1 Typical Parcel Movement from Origin to Destination	129
#2 Key Financials (2009 & 2010)	131
#3 Exterior Packaging Materials	133
#4 Comparative Securing Systems	135
#5 How to Read UN Markings	137
#6 Parcel Delivery Providers	139
#7 Oversize Parcels	143
#8 Shipping Zone Rates	145
#9 Contract Terminology	147
#10 Contracting Cycle	151

SECTION V – GLOSSARY SHIPPING TERMS **153**

SECTION VI – NOTES **171**

Index **185**

Figures

#1 Product Distribution Models	29
#2 Bar Code (1D and 2D) Comparison	33
#3 EPC RFID Tag	35
#4 Box Flap Adhesive	52
#5 Banding (or Strapping)	53
#6 Staple Closure Methods	53
#7 Center Seam and H-seal Box Closure Methods	55
#8 Addressing Your Parcel	56
#9 Traditional Insulating Materials versus Equivalent VIP	58
#10 Class 9, Dry Ice Label and Markings	60
#11 UN Hazmat Marking	64
#12 Oxidizing Materials Label	66
#13 Example Shipping Paper – Benzene	67
#14 Basic Pallet Design	75
#15 Corrugated Fluting	77
#16 Regular Slotted Container (RSC)	78
#17 Flat Mailers	78
#18 Folders	79
#19 Box Dimensions	80
#20 Types of BMCs	82
#21 BMC Basic Rules	82
#22 How to Measure Length and Girth	110
#23 Cubic Size Calculations	112

Tables

#1 Key Carrier Service Levels	14
#2 Residential or Commercial Delivery Classification	15
#3 International Parcel Delivery Options	16
#4 Market Matrix	20
#5 Characteristics of Traditional and E-commerce Delivery	30
#6 Average Amounts of Dry Ice Usage	60
#7 Packing Groups	68
#8 Box Strength Guidelines	80
#9 Drop Height Test	89
#10 Domestic Ground Commercial Rates	96
#11 Weight and Size Limits	110
#12 Oversized Ground Delivery Parcels	111
#13 What Freight Loss and Damage Really Cost	118

Introduction

TRANSPORTING PARCELS, small packages, and express letter shipments has grown to be a significant segment of the transportation industry, larger than the airline, pipeline, and railroad industries. The parcel and small package delivery industry has grown from a small part of U.S. freight transportation to become a major component. In fact, this market has been the fastest-growing transportation segment in the United States over the past two decades and now accounts for over 10 percent of the gross domestic product.

Industry observers believe there are two fundamental reasons the parcel and small package delivery industry has become so important in recent years. One reason cited was the change in production and distribution methods. The second reason is the industry itself, which is at the vanguard of transportation delivery modernization.

Material presented in this book provides an overview of the parcel and small package delivery industry and its importance to the economy. The intent is to present and identify old patterns as well as recognize new trends to give readers a better understanding of the industry's marketplace. This book includes information gathered and compiled from a myriad of sources and the author's knowledge and work experience in the industry.

SECTION I – PARCEL DELIVERY ENVIRONMENT

    1.0   Importance of Parcel Delivery Service

    1.1   Role of Parcel Carriers

    1.2   Typical Carrier System

    1.3   Dominant Carriers

    1.4   Delivery Options

    1.5   Parcel Classification

    1.6   Types of Loads

    1.7   Shipping Hazards

    1.8   Industry's Competitive Structure

    1.9   LTL Sector

    1.10 Parcel Consolidators

    1.11 Electronic Commerce (E-commerce)

    1.12 Dynamics of Home Delivery

    1.13 Wireless Information Technology

    1.14 Sortation Systems Technology

    1.15 Global Environment

SECTION I

PARCEL DELIVERY ENVIRONMENT

THERE IS NO UNIFORM definition of *parcel (or small package) delivery*. However, a common definition used is the flow of goods between different people or organizations, at different locations.[1] This definition excludes movements carried out by a firm of their own goods within a single plant or business location. Many companies call themselves a parcel delivery carrier and provide service offerings different from those of traditional transport carriers.

The parcel delivery industry consist of carriers or organizations that transport shipments larger than a single letter but small enough for one person to handle without support. Important features of the industry are carrier pickup at origin and carrier delivery at destination. Parcel delivery is inherently multimodal, using a small truck, auto, or messenger for pickup and delivery, and another mode of transport such as truck, rail, or air for the line-haul.

Two carriers instrumental in developing the parcel delivery industry, REA Express and Purolator Courier, have since vanished.[2] REA Express operated between 1918 and 1975, and during its heyday was the largest ground and air express transport service. REA Express began as the American Railroad Express Company after the U.S. government nationalized private express carriers and the railroads. Privatized by the end of World War I, eighty-six (86) of the country's railroads created a private company named Railroad Express Agency (REA). REA acquired the American Railway Express Company and placed it back in private hands. American Railway Express's name changed to REA Express in 1970. Poor management, strikes by employees, and competition from private carriers and the United States Postal Service led REA Express to file for bankruptcy in 1975. Purolator Courier performed ground and air courier service in the U.S. starting in the 1960s. In 1987, Emery acquired Purolator's U.S. operation and Onyx Corporation acquired Purolator's Canada operation, which they later sold to Canada Post. One year after taking over Emery, CNF Corporation closed its U.S. Purolator subsidiary.

1.0 Importance of Parcel Delivery Service

A question often asked is *Why has parcel delivery service become so important in recent years?* There are two fundamental reasons often cited: first, businesses produce and distribute goods and services, and second, the uniqueness of services offered by parcel carriers. A change in production and distribution has created a trend toward reducing inventories and rapid customer response. Parcel carriers have been at the forefront of providing time-definite, fast delivery service. Emphasis on reducing inventories, to reduce overhead cost of manufacturing and distributing goods, has resulted in the need for faster delivery. Introducing customized products has resulted in supply chains that depend on make-to-order, or rapid replenishment of goods, to avoid shortages and excess inventories. Cost-savings and increased customer value require rapid transport, time-definite delivery, and the need to transport small quantities of the right commodities to the right locations.

Parcel carriers do not simply load parcels onto a truck and transport them from one location to another. Carriers also provide an array of related services designed to improve the value of their customers' products and services. Parcel carriers are instrumental in bringing together the different modes of transport to provide various delivery services at the least cost. Intermodal service has expanded to other areas of transport, with truck carriers sending their trailers, loaded with cargo, long distances by rail and ocean carriers. Integrated transport service has fostered a change in production and distribution, which has resulted in lower costs to deliver goods to consumers. Additionally, and often critical to customers is the need to track their shipment from pick up to delivery. Delivery of information by Internet or Electronic Data Exchange is a value-added service commonly provided by parcel carriers.

1.1 Role of Parcel Carriers

Ideally, transport keeps goods moving rapidly and reliably, and does not delay shipments to accumulate an entire truckload or railcar of cargo. It is the role of parcel carriers to provide an efficient transport service to move goods individually, or in batches, quickly and reliably. Parcel carriers also provide essential services, such as shipment tracking, pickup, and delivery at the customer's address, and integration of information flow between shipper and receiver. During the past two decades, the explosive growth in the number of parcels transported has transformed the domestic parcel delivery industry and its impact on freight transport. Parcel carriers have played a key role in the U.S. economy by transporting time-sensitive shipments critical to the competitiveness of U.S. businesses both domestically and internationally.

There are four trends, which reflect society's reliance on parcel carriers—mass customization, inventory reduction, advanced technology, and core competencies.[3]

Mass customization is the model that replaced mass production. M. M. Tseng and J. Jiao defined mass customization as "producing goods and services to meet individual customer's needs with near mass production efficiency." An example of mass customization is shoppers at a Levi jean outlet can have their measurements entered into Levi's computer system and transmitted to a Levi plant for manufacture. Mass customization is equally appropriate for small businesses in that it is not dependent on economies of scale.[4] Parcel delivery service is important in that no other mode of transport can handle a small shipment at such a reasonable cost, and offer guaranteed delivery with an authenticated receipt of delivery. In addition, parcel carriers perform both "order taking" and "order distribution" tasks.

Often, inventory is the single largest asset many companies possess. While inventory consumes space and is susceptible to damage and obsolescence it is an important component of the business cycle. Another trend that encourages greater use of parcel service is the need to reduce inventories of manufactured products, referred to as **inventory reduction**. The most efficient way for businesses to reduce inventory is by reducing the time it takes for them to deliver a customer's order. Parcel delivery service helps to reduce inventories by providing a fast and reliable service. Reliable service also reduces the need for safety stocks to protect against late deliveries.

A third trend is the increasing use of **advanced technology** in most areas of the economy. High tech equipment is expensive, and as a result, parcel carriers often deliver it. Often, companies need replacement parts immediately. Parcel carriers, with guaranteed same-day and next-day services often provide the transport and have been the leaders in the express transportation industry. In the late 1970s, FedEx established a toll-free number so its customers could track the progress of their shipments.[5] In 1994, FedEx launched fedex.com as the first transportation website to offer customers online shipment tracking.

Core competencies are things that a firm does well and which meet the following three conditions:[6] (1) provides consumer benefits (2) is not easy for competitors to imitate, and (3) is widely leveraged to many products, services, and markets. An example is UPS's entry into secure Internet document exchange. In partnership with Hewlett-Packard, in May 1999, UPS began offering UPS Document Exchange. The service was designed to send paper-based documents across the Internet to multiple recipients. Another example was UPS's entry into the flow of funds. This service expanded the flow of information support, associated with delivery, to the flow of payment support. Services offered by parcel carriers enable firms to focus on their core competencies.

1.1.1 CARGO TRANSPORTED

Another measure of parcel carriers' importance is to examine what they deliver. The Bureau of Transportation Statistics' *Commodity Flow Survey* provides this information and confirms the growing importance of parcel delivery service to the economy. Growth from 1993 to

1997 was extraordinary, and parcel carriers' share of shipment value grew from 9.6 percent to 12.0 percent. The 2002 survey showed parcel carriers share slipping to 11.8 percent. By 2007, parcel carriers share had rebounded to 13.4 percent.[7] Goods transported by parcel carriers read like a list of products used in many of the fastest growing industries:

- Pharmaceuticals
- Medical supplies
- Chemicals
- Plastics
- Electronics products
- Computers and related equipment
- Precision instruments
- Printed matter
- Apparel
- Repair parts

NOTE: Parcel carriers deliver many goods not included in the *Commodity Flow Survey*, such as contracts, legal documents, and copy for printed material.

1.1.2 IMPACT ON RETAILING

Retailing continues to undergo a transformation, evidenced by the growth in e-commerce, where customers place their order by Internet or telephone and have it delivered directly to them. Future growth of retail e-commerce promises to have an impact that rivals the massive changes that have affected retailing in the last seventy years. There was a shift from the multilayered, fixed-price selling chains with downtown stores to emerging, large, suburban stores in the 1950s and 60s.[8] Following in the 1980s and 1990s were large retailers who cut out intermediaries and reduced the price of many retail goods. No longer is physical proximity the most important consideration. Increasingly, electronic shipping and ordering has replaced the trip to the store, and parcel delivery service has replaced the return trip home with the goods. Therefore, growth in e-commerce has parcel carriers constantly searching for innovative ways to provide services.

1.2 Typical Carrier System[9]

The technology of providing parcel delivery service is unique. Parcel carriers aggregate parcels into larger units in order to move them at a reasonable cost. *Aggregation* and *disaggregation* define how parcel carriers operate. Starting with a simple parcel service that uses only road transport, the task of delivery goes as follows. A parcel carrier driver, using a small *local area* vehicle, picks up multiple parcels at various origins and delivers them to an *origin hub* or terminal. At the origin hub, workers sort shipments by outbound line-haul truck destinations. After loading, line-haul trucks depart for the next *hub* or terminal on the parcel's route, where workers again unload and sort the parcels. If this is the *destination hub* of all the parcels on the truck, workers will sort the parcels and load them onto local area vehicles for delivery. If there are not enough parcels to fill a line-haul truck for each possible destination hub, the truck will carry parcels to *intermediate hubs* for further sorting until they reach their destination hubs (see Appendix 1, Typical Parcel Movement from Origin to Destination).

While major parcel delivery carriers operate their own pickup and delivery services, they often use other transport companies for the line-haul move. The United States Postal Service is a major user of commercial truck carrier services for its line-haul movements. Railroads provide line-haul services and become part of the movement, both to carry truck trailers (piggyback service) and to carry containers (essentially truck trailers without wheels). Parcels requiring "overnight" and "second-day" service rely on aircraft instead of trucks for the line-haul to meet delivery time guarantees. If parcels are moving over a short distance, the line-haul is usually accomplished by truck, as it is cheaper than air. This is true even if the name of the service includes the word "air." Generally, a shipper's main concern is not the mode of transport, but if the delivery will be on time and intact.

1.2.1 FINANCIAL COMPARISON

Financially strong companies have important advantages over financially weak competitors. First, carriers with capital are more likely to invest in their organization and offer the broadest scope of services and geographical reach. Second, financially strong carriers have a lower cost of capital than those with weaker finances. Third, financially strong carriers can afford to wait longer for investments to pay off than their financially weaker competitors.

1.2.2 OPERATING COMPARISONS

Major parcel carriers use hub-and-spoke terminals to delivery both ground and air shipments.

Primary air hubs are located in Memphis, TN (FedEx); Louisville, KY (UPS); and Indianapolis, IN (USPS). FedEx and UPS use their air hubs to handle express volumes. USPS uses FedEx hubs for shipments hauled under contract. Carriers use local distribution centers to make the final delivery. The primary difference in carrier networks revolves around their ground delivery. A ground shipment involves various modes of transportation and can take two to five days for delivery. Both UPS and USPS have long-standing ground delivery networks that handle large volumes.

1.2.3 WORKFORCE CHARACTERISTICS

Parcel delivery carriers use an array of employees and contractors to delivery parcels. Parcel carriers' workforce characteristics influence their ability to control labor cost. Carriers with a high concentration of unionized employees are less flexible and generally have higher unit labor costs. The Teamsters Union represents many UPS employees who deliver, transport, and sort parcels. In all, four unions (American Postal Workers Union, National Postal Mail Handlers, National Association of Letter Carriers, and National Rural Letter Carriers Association) represent postal workers who sort, transport, and deliver parcels. USPS contracts for transport and delivery services in many rural locations. FedEx Express delivery personnel are mainly nonunion contractors who provide much of the ground delivery service.

1.2.4 VARIABLE VERSES FIXED NETWORKS

Carriers' unit costs are high when volume is low and their network costs are fixed. Internal use of assets to provide services cause networks to be less flexible. Capital required to purchase assets (e.g., airplanes, delivery vehicles) and build sortation hubs can be substantial. Fixed network carriers are those who own and operate their own airline. Major carriers also invest heavily in their sortation facilities. The United States Postal Service purchases air, rail, and truck transport under long-term contracts. This network has a variable cost characteristic. Carriers that employ personnel to transport, sort, and deliver parcels have high short-term fixed costs. UPS and FedEx employ most of their sortation employees part-time, which allows them labor-cost flexibility. On the other hand, USPS has the least amount of flexibility because most of its sortation employees have full-time status. FedEx Ground uses contractors extensively for delivery and this cost depends on the number of parcels delivered.

1.2.5 INTEGRATED NETWORKS

Integrated networks delivery parcel products, from overnight to ground delivery service, using the same local resources and delivery routes. Typically, a major parcel carrier will use three separate delivery networks. First, it operates a network for *air express shipments*. Second, it operates a ground network for *business delivery* locations. Third, it operates a ground network for *home deliveries*.

1.2.6 JOINT-LINE VERSES SINGLE-LINE SERVICE

Joint-line service can differ significantly from single-line service. With single-line service, the customer understands that a single carrier will be responsible for the end-to-end transport. In joint-line service, two or more carriers provide the service. Joint-line service requires a physical transfer of the shipment as well as the legal responsibility for carriage. The origin and destination carriers negotiate terms of transfer and payment for services to the destination carrier. The Postal Rate Commission regulates the price paid to USPS for services it provides as part of a joint-line service. Parcel carriers provide domestic express and deferred air delivery as a single-line service. USPS's commercial ground parcel service is joint-line and the service provided retail customers is single-line.

1.3 Dominant Carriers

Measured by revenue, parcel delivery service has been the fastest growing segment of the freight transport business in the United States for the past three decades. Year 2005 was a solid year for the domestic industry, paced by an impressive performance by USPS. Three large carriers—FedEx Corporation (FedEx), United Parcel Service (UPS), and United States Postal Service (USPS)—dominate the United States parcel industry. These three carriers account for over 90 percent of all domestic parcel shipments and revenue. There are multistate (regional) parcel carriers who also offer services. (see Appendix 2, Key Financials).

1.3.1 UNITED PARCEL SERVICE (UPS)

UPS is the world's largest parcel delivery carrier in terms of both revenue and volume. UPS originated (1907) in Seattle, Washington, as the American Messenger Company and is currently based in Atlanta, GA (since 1991). UPS operates the largest single transport network in the world. The infrastructure of UPS is extensive and includes a fleet of about 93,000 motor vehicles and 268 aircraft going to 391 airports in the USA and 219 abroad. UPS has use of a large fleet of aircraft, making it the second largest freight airline in the world.[10] UPS handles 4.0 billion parcels annually.

UPS purchased Menlo Worldwide Forwarding in 2004. Menlo provides value-added supply chain services that focus on moving heavyweight freight for commercial, industrial, and government customers worldwide. Overnite officially became *UPS Freight* in 2006. This allowed UPS to expand its less-than-truckload operation. Another primary business service is time-definite delivery of parcels and documents. UPS is the industry leader in the delivery of goods purchased over the Internet. UPS delivers more than 6 percent of the United States Gross Domestic Product.

UPS Operating Units:[11]

UPS Supply Chain Solutions: Distribution, logistics, transport (ocean, rail, air, and truck), freight forwarding, international trade management, customs brokerage, supply chain design, and service parts logistics

UPS Capital: Unit specializes in financial solutions

UPS Consulting: Provides consultation related to moving goods, information, and funds

UPS Mail Innovations: Provides expedited mail service for flats, bound printed material, and irregular parcels (mail typically larger than a letter but less than a one-pound parcel). As mail nears its final destination, it is funneled into a USPS facility.

UPS Office (formerly, Mail Boxes Etc.): In April 2001, UPS acquired MBE, a franchiser of independently owned and operated retail shipping and business services.

Historically, UPS only faced competition from USPS for the inexpensive ground-based delivery market. FedEx expanded into the ground market by acquiring RPS (originally Roadway Package System) and renamed it FedEx Ground. Parcel service within the United States generated most of UPS's revenue, 62.1 percent, or $28.16 billion, in 2009.[12] International shipping generated 22 percent, or $11.29 billion, of UPS's revenue in 2008. In 2009, UPS Freight, Supply Chain Solutions, and other auxiliary businesses generated $7.44 billion or 16.5 percent of UPS's revenue. While guarding its 54 percent ground-market share, UPS seeks to capture market share in the express market. UPS holds 36 percent of the express market, while its primary competitor, FedEx, holds 49 percent. The worldwide recession in 2008 and 2009 negatively affected UPS's domestic packaging, international packaging, and supply chain and freight segments. As the global economy began its recovery, volume and revenue trends began to improve in the latter half of 2009.

1.3.2 FEDEX CORPORATION (FEDEX)

FedEx started as Federal Express in 1971 by former U.S. Marine Frederick W. Smith in Little Rock, Arkansas, but moved to Memphis, Tennessee, in 1973.[13] In August 1989, the company acquired Flying Tigers, an international cargo airline. It inherited Flying Tiger's U.S. military transport contract and carried passengers between the continental United States and overseas installations until October 1992. In January 1998, Federal Express acquired Caliber System, Inc., which owned Roadway Package System (RPS), Roberts Express, Viking Freight, and Caliber Logistics. When these companies merged, the new organization became FDX Corp. The name "FedEx," an unofficial abbreviation for Federal Express, became the company's primary brand name in 1994. In February 2004, FedEx acquired Kinko's, a chain that provides printing and business services. FDX Corporation changed its name to FedEx Corporation in 2000 and dropped the name "Federal Express."

In 2001, FedEx acquired American Freightways and combined operations with Viking Freight to create FedEx Freight. FedEx offers overnight courier, ground, heavy freight, logistics services, and document copying. FedEx, the first parcel carrier to use jet airlines for its services expanded after deregulation of the cargo airline industry. FedEx's use of the hub-spoke distribution model in airfreight enabled it to become a world leader in its field. The company operates much of its domestic overnight freight business through the Memphis hub. FedEx organized into operating units, each of which has its own version of FedEx logo. In all versions, the Fed is purple and the Ex is a different color for each division. The corporate logo Ex is gray.

FedEx Operating Units:[14]

FedEx Express. This service uses a large fleet of aircraft and local delivery trucks to move parcels. *Ex* color is orange.

FedEx Ground. Service is slower and cheaper compared with FedEx Express. Independent contractors own and operate their own trucks. *Ex* color is green.
- FedEx Home Delivery – Delivery to residences
- FedEx SmartPost – This unit consolidates parcels

FedEx Freight. Less-than-truckload (LTL) freight services. *Ex* color is red.
- FedEx Freight East – formerly American Freightways
- FedEx Freight West – formerly Viking Freight
- Caribbean Transport Services – airfreight services to the Caribbean islands

FedEx Office (formerly, Kinko's). Provides media services such as, printing, copying, Internet service, and a central location to deposit parcels for shipping. *Ex* color is blue.

FedEx Custom Critical. This unit delivers urgent, valuable, and hazardous items. *Passport Transport* – transports cars, mainly high value. Drivers are independent contractors. *Ex* color is blue.

FedEx Trade Networks. Provides customs, insurance, and transportation consulting services. *Ex* color is yellow.

FedEx Supply Chain Services. Provides logistics services. *Ex* color is gray.

FedEx Services. Provides marketing and information technology services. *Ex* color is gray.

UPS and USPS are FedEx's major competitors. FedEx also competes in freight forwarding service, logistics service, and the trucking sector. FedEx is the clear market leader in express shipping with 49 percent market share by volume in the United States.[15] In ground shipping, FedEx is striving to establish itself in a market dominated by UPS.

FedEx Ground, which accounts for 20 percent of FedEx's total revenue, offers parcel delivery service throughout the United States, Canada, and Puerto Rico. FedEx Freight provides less-than-truckload (LTL) freight service and accounts for 12 percent of FedEx's total revenue. FedEx Services (FedEx Office) generates 5 percent of FedEx's total revenue. Like most other carriers, FedEx had a poor fiscal year in 2009 with revenue decreasing from $37.953 billion in 2008 to $35.497 billion. While FedEx Ground revenue increased, the overall decline in revenue was largely because of decreased domestic and international sales.

1.3.3 UNITED STATES POSTAL SERVICE (USPS)[16]

USPS was created to process and deliver mail to individuals and businesses in the United States. The Postal Reorganization Act (39 U.S.C.A. § 101 et seq.) created the postal service as an independent establishment of the executive branch on August 12, 1970. USPS began operations on July 1, 1971, replacing the Post Office Department. The organization consists of regional and field division offices that together supervise 37,683 post offices, branches, and stations. The postmaster general is the chief executive officer, appointed by the nine governors of the Postal Service. The nine governors are appointed by the president of the United States, with the advice and consent of the Senate. The governors and the postmaster general appoint the deputy postmaster general. These eleven people constitute the board of governors.

USPS Facilities:

- A Main Post Office is the primary postal facility in a community.
- A Post Office Station is not the main post office, but serves a community.
- A Post Office Branch is a main post office found outside a community.
- A Classified Unit is a station or branch operated by USPS employees.
- A Contract Postal Unit is a station or branch operated by an independent contractor.
- A Finance Unit is a station or branch that provides window service and accepts mail, but does not make deliveries.
- A Processing and Distribution Center (P&DC) is a mail facility that processes mail to and from a designated service area.
- A Sectional Center Facility is a P&DC for a designated geographical area defined by one or more three-digit ZIP code prefixes.
- A Bulk Mail Center (BMC) is a mail facility that processes bulk rate parcels and serves as the *hub* in a hub-and-spoke network.
- An Auxiliary Sorting Facility (ASF) is a mail facility that processes bulk rate parcels and serves as the *spoke* in a hub-and-spoke network.

USPS Products and Services:

First-Class Mail. Mail service used by individuals and businesses where one rate applies

Standard Mail. Used mainly by businesses. The mailing must be a minimum of two hundred pieces, and each piece must weigh less than 1 lb. (454 g). There is an annual fee for this service.

Bulk Mail. Used by businesses to send large quantities of mail through a Bulk Mail Entry Unit post office at a discount

Parcel Post. Mail service used to send parcels weighing up to seventy pounds (31.75 kg). Rates are determined by space occupied, distance traveled, and weight.

Media Mail. Mail service used to send items such as, books, printed material, diskettes, CDs, sound recordings, and videotapes. Maximum allowable weight is seventy pounds (31.75 kg).

Library Mail. Same as media mail, but receives an additional discount. Used to mail books and recordings to and from public libraries, museums, and academic institutions.

Priority Mail. This is an expedited delivery service. Average delivery time is two to three days (not guaranteed). A parcel can weigh up to seventy pounds (31.75 kg).

Express Mail. This is the fastest mail service. Typically, overnight or second-day-guaranteed delivery. A parcel can weigh up to fifty pounds (22.7 kg).

Global Services. Airmail, Global Priority, Global Express, and Global Express Guaranteed Mail services ship mail and parcels to almost every country and territory.

Airline and Rail Division. USPS does not own or operate any aircraft or trains. Mail is transported on airlines that have contractual agreements with USPS. USPS also contracts with Amtrak to carry mail between cities.

Add-on Services. The Postal Service offers additional services for some types of mail: delivery confirmation, signature confirmation, insurance, certified mail, registered mail, collect on delivery (COD), and postage stamps.

USPS enjoys a government monopoly on most first-class mail and standard mail (formerly called third-class mail), as described in the Private Express Statutes. USPS also enjoys monopoly privilege in placing mail into standard mailboxes marked "U.S. Mail." Private carriers must deliver parcels direct to the recipient, leave them in the open near the recipient's door, or place them in a special box dedicated solely to that carrier. USPS's 2009 fiscal year-end financial results showed a net loss of $3.8 billion dollars.[17] Total mail volume in 2009 was 177.1 billion pieces compared with 202.7 billion pieces in 2008, a decline of 12.7 percent. Competition from e-mail, UPS, and FedEx has forced USPS to adjust its business strategy and modernize products and services.

1.4 Delivery Options

Major parcel carriers offer in-transit service variations (travel time from origin to destination). Carriers state in-transit delivery time in terms such as "next morning before 8:30 AM," "before noon," or second day before noon." This requires a deadline for shippers to give their parcels to the carrier. The carrier can pick up parcels at the shipper's location, the shipper can place parcels in the carrier's drop box, or the shipper can deliver parcels to the carrier's facility. There are service options offered without a specified delivery guarantee that have a known delivery time. An example would be USPS's Priority Mail, which generally delivers goods to most addresses in the U.S. within two business days.

1.4.1. DOMESTIC SERVICE OFFERINGS

There can be a significant cost difference between service levels. A parcel sent "next day" would cost more than the same parcel sent "ground." Other service levels include sameday, international hundredweight, and multiweight service levels. The first step a shipper should take in identifying shipping costs is to look at the required service level. Parcel carriers typically call their different offerings service levels. FedEx Priority Overnight and UPS Ground are examples of carrier service levels. Carriers typically group service levels by express and ground categories, as shown in Table 1, Key Carrier Service Levels.

Table 1: Key Carrier Service Levels

	Grouping	Service Level	Standard Delivery Times
Express	Next-Day	Early AM First Overnight Next-day Air	8 AM to most major cities, 8:30 to 9 AM in others, 10 AM to remote areas
		Priority Overnight Next-day 10:30 AM	10:30 AM to most U.S. zip codes, 12 PM or 5 PM in remote areas
		Next-day Air Saver Standard Overnight Next-day 3 PM	3 PM to most commercial locations and 4:30 PM to remote locations
	2-Day	2-day Air AM	10:30 AM to most U.S. zip codes, 12 PM in remote areas
		2-day Air	End of Business Day (5 PM), 7 PM to residential locations
	3-Day	3-day Select	End of Business Day (5 PM)
		Express Saver	4:30 PM to commercial locations, 7 PM to residential locations

| | Ground | Ground (UPS) Ground (FedEx) | 3 to 5 PM Business Days, depending on destination zip, 5 PM for commercial locations |

Source: Data compiled from FedEx web site, http://www.fedex.com/us/services/deliveryoptions.html and UPS website, http://ups.com/using/svc-index.html, accessed June 2009.

The term *residential* delivery refers to noncommercial or private residences, apartments, farms, estates, dormitories, home-based businesses, ranches, rectories, parsonages, or other locations where the entire premises on which a dwelling for living is not open to the walk-in public during normal business hours.[18] One way to avoid a residential delivery fee is to deliver or pick up the shipment at the carrier's terminal, when possible (see Table 2, Residential or Commercial Delivery Classification).

Table 2: Residential or Commercial Delivery Classification

Commercial	Residence
Nursing home	Rectory
Funeral home	Convent
Church	Parsonage
Prison	A residence where products are sold or distributed
Firehouse	Residents of multiple-unit dwellings, such as: • Apartment buildings • Condominiums • College dormitories
Farm	
Dental/medical/veterinary office	
Insurance agency	
Retail shop	
Administrative offices and buildings of schools	

Source: Adapted from FedEx web site, http://www.fedex.com/us/services/us/homedelivery/index.html, accessed June 2008.

1.4.2 INTERNATIONAL DELIVERY SERVICES

Carriers offer value-added services designed to assist customers in improving their supply chain. Services include warehousing and order fulfillment, electronic information exchange, and financial transaction processing a modern version of the old concept of cash-on-delivery. Table 3, International Parcel Delivery Options, is representative of international services offered by FedEx, UPS, and USPS. There is a trade-off between speed of delivery and cost of delivery. The effect of distance on cost has a greater impact than weight. A substantial premium is paid for speed.

Table 3: International Parcel Delivery Options

Carrier	Option	Feature
UPS	Worldwide Express Plus	2nd-day delivery by 8:30 or 9:00 AM to Europe and Canada
	Worldwide Expedited	3rd-day delivery to Mexico and Canada and 4 to 5-day delivery to Europe and Asia
	Standard to Canada	low-cost, guaranteed ground delivery
FEDEX	International First	2nd-day delivery by 8 or 8:30 AM to select European cities
	International Economy	2 to 5 days – based on country
	International Ground	3 to 7 days – delivery to Canada and Puerto Rico
USPS	Global Express Guaranteed	1 to 3 business days – date certain delivery to over 190 countries
	Priority Mail International	6 to 10 business days – reliable, priority handling to over 190 countries
	First-Class Mail International	Varies by destination – economic way to send items 4 pounds or less

Source: Data compiled from FedEx web site, http://www.fedex.com/us/services/deliveryoptions.html, UPS web site, http://www.ups.com/using/svc-index.html, and United States Postal Service web site, http://www.usps.com/international/sendpackages.htm, accessed June 2008.

Timely arrival of a shipment is often essential to a customer's business operation. A good example of this is a repair part for a machine that is on an assembly line. Often, the value of on-time delivery is greater than the retail value of the part and its freight charge. Customers regard the ability to track their shipments—commonly referred to as in-transit visibility—as essential. Technological advances, such as bar code scanners, electronic exchange of information, satellite tracking of vehicles, and satellite mobile phone communication have enhanced shippers' ability to track their shipments. Carriers' tracking features enable shippers to gauge the arrival time of their shipment.

1.5 Parcel Classification

Parcel carriers often referred to as *integrated carriers*; integrate the operations of different modes of transportation, such as rail, air, and road transport, to provide their service. Major carriers such as FedEx and UPS rely on a "hub-and-spoke" network to transport and sort parcels. Within each hub or operating center, parcels may travel through the system in one of three ways, depending on the characteristics and classification of the packaging – *small*, *regular*, or *irregular* shipping unit.[19]

Smalls are parcels less than 450 cubic inches and ten pounds. Because of the difficulty in handling small-size parcels, carriers often consolidated them. It is common for smalls to go through a sort that consolidates them into a bag containing numerous parcels addressed to the same geographic location.

Regular shipping units are containers typically larger than 450 cubic inches and weighing ten to seventy-five pounds. Carriers sort regular parcels on conveyor network systems.

Irregular shipping units have unique characteristics that prevent the use of high volume conveyor systems. These shipping units are:

- only partially encased in corrugated fiberboard;
- packaged in plastic, metal, or wood on its exterior surface;
- tubular or round;
- not packaged in a shipping container; and/or
- oversized, or weigh more than seventy-five pounds.

Carriers use slower moving conveyors, carts, or pallets to sort and move irregular shipping units through their hubs and onto outbound trucks or aircraft. During short distance shipments (300 miles or less), carriers may load and reload parcels as many as five times and send them through three different sorts. Sorts include manual, mechanical, or automated handling on high-speed belts, slides, chutes, and rollers, which presents hazards. Hazards can cause damage if packaging does not provide adequate protection.

1.6 Types of Loads

Load type depends on the contents, degree of protection, and strength of the packaging used. General terminology used in the packaging and transportation industries to describe the types of shipping loads is, *easy*, *average*, and *difficult*.[20]

An **easy** load is one that contains items of moderate density (up to 15 pounds per cubic foot) and fills a container, or is packaged in interior containers that fill the outer mailing container. Puncture or shock will not normally damage an easy load, cause it to shift, move in the container, or present a hazard to other parcels.

An **average** load is one that contains moderately concentrated items packed directly into a shipping container. Packaging provides partial support to all surfaces of the container. Items are nested within partitions or in separate paperboard boxes to prevent shifting and damage.

A **difficult** load is one that contains items that require a high degree of protection to prevent puncture, distortion, or shock to the items or packaging. Fragile objects, high-density items, delicate instruments, and small bulk items that do not support the mailing container are not acceptable in paperboard boxes, bags, or wraps.

1.7 Shipping Hazards

The parcel delivery environment consists of mechanical sortation systems and manual single parcel handling. In addition to the normal shipping hazards found in truckload, LTL truck, railroad, and airfreight, parcel shipping includes unique hazards. Often, hazards are more severe because of automated sorting and handling equipment used by ground and air express carriers. There are many hazards in this environment, but the main ones are *shock, vibration, compression, extreme climate conditions, and altitude*.[21]

Shock to parcels can occur if dropped, struck by other parcels or objects during the sorting operation, or if they shift or fall during transit. Impact creates shock, which may cause fatigue or damage to parcels and their contents. From a package-engineering standpoint, it is critical to design parcels to withstand shock from all directions. Because of automated sorting systems, parcel carriers cannot always honor orientation or shock labels, or "keep upright" arrows. Generally, parcels will travel in the most stable orientation, which is the parcel's lowest center of gravity. This helps prevent parcels from tumbling down chutes and slides, or from falling over during loading or sorting.

Vibration occurs during parcel sorting. Automated sorting can create low-level vibration at a constant frequency into parcels as they move on conveyor systems. Mechanical sorting with forklifts will induce vibration, usually at a low frequency, as parcels bounce on pallets or forklift blades during transit. Manual sorting induces no noticeable vibration. In-transit motions subject parcels to many levels of vibration. Typically, aircraft induced vibration is high frequency and low amplitude. Truckload and trailer on flatbed railcar (TOFC) will subject the parcels to lower frequencies, but at much higher amplitudes than aircraft. This can result in damage such as scuffing, abrasion, loosening of fasteners and closures, and fatigue.

Compression may be a static condition, as in a trailer or aircraft, when the vehicle is not moving and the parcel is under load from other parcels. Alternatively, compression may be a dynamic condition that occurs when the trailer or aircraft is in motion. Dynamic compression will impose both vertical and lateral compressive forces. Frequently, stacking is unavoidable because of space and time constraints. Handlers may use an interlocking method rather than column stacking when loading parcels into trailers or aircraft containers, usually building a "wall" across the trailer or container. Interlocking reduces corrugated box stacking strength up to 50 percent compared with column stacking. Interlocking patterns are more stable and better suited for random size boxes.

Sorting operations result in a lower level of compression force than in-transit movement, except when jam-ups occur in automated sorting systems. Jam-ups can create a large dynamic compression force as heavier parcels slide into and build-up behind other parcels. Another instance of high compressive force occurs when workers use pallets and forklifts to sort, load, and unload parcels. This can occur when parcels overhang the pallet and push into another pallet or against a vehicle or container wall. Stacked pallets can also create compression. A loaded pallet with bottom deckboards will cause less damage to a load below it compared with a pallet that has no bottom deckboards. A pallet with a full bottom deck provides the best load support.

Climate conditions that can cause damage are high or low temperatures and high humidity. Carrier feeder-aircraft and parcel delivery vehicles expose parcels to the same temperature and humidity inside and outside the vehicle. Temperatures can range from a high of 140° F to a low of −50° F inside the vehicle, and relative humidity as high as 100 percent. The exception is when a parcel is inside large cargo aircraft that maintain an appropriate temperature.

Altitude can be problematic on feeder-aircraft not pressurized. Large cargo jets pressurize to approximately 8,000 feet. Over-the-road altitudes should not exceed 12,000 feet at the extreme.

Other conditions include orientation of parcels when tilted on inclines and in flight, and the "bridging" of long parcels in automated sorting systems. Bridging occurs when a long parcel is jammed near its ends on a conveyor or chute during the sorting operation. A parcel struck near the center by fast moving parcels can incur damage. Automated sorting does not maintain a single orientation—inclines and slopes are inevitable. Conveyor angles can range from 12° to 37° and slides may range from 17° to 30°. To prevent possible damage, use containers designed to traverse incline angles.

1.8 Industry's Competitive Structure[22]

Originally, the choice of parcel carriers was limited to USPS or UPS. Federal Express entered the market with an overnight delivery service and Roadway Package System (currently FedEx Ground). Federal Express was the first carrier to offer parcel-tracking capability. Later, Airborne Express and DHL Worldwide Express entered domestic service. Today, parcel carriers are getting stiff competition from less-than-truckload (LTL) carriers. LTL carriers have adjusted their networks and upgraded their systems in order to offer time-definite delivery and shipment tracking. Because of stiff competition, shippers now have more options, not only among parcel carriers, but among LTL competitors and consolidators as well. To understand parcel-shipping choices, it is helpful for consumers to consider how competitors match up. Four factors define parcel delivery: origin and destination, consumer requirements, delivery speed, and shape and weight.

1.8.1 ORIGIN AND DESTINATION

The origin and destination determine delivery difficulty and the effort required to attract customers. Table 4 illustrates a typical two-by-two matrix involving businesses and consumers. An example of a *business-consumer* (B2C) initiative is Amazon.com, which sells products over the Internet directly to the buyer. On the other hand, ChemConnect.com and Chemdex.com, who deal with chemicals, are *business-business* (B2B) initiatives that bring firms together in the virtual marketplace. Typically, B2B initiatives involve many participants with complex rules, higher purchasing amounts, and complex products that require greater certainty regarding order fulfillment. *Consumer-originating* markets require a retail infrastructure or on-demand pickup capability that accepts individual parcels. This market also includes occasional small business customers. *Business-originating* markets include markets where regular pickups justify a higher degree of hands on sales effort. These markets involve carriers who offer specific customer pricing.

Table 4: Market Matrix

Shipment Destination	SHIPMENT ORIGIN	
	Business	Consumer
Business	B-B	B-C
Consumer	C-B	C-C

1.8.2 CONSUMER REQUIREMENTS

A key process carriers use to divide markets is to look at the attention customers require and the attention they are willing to provide. Parcel volume is important to carriers because it directly affects their pick up costs. Generally, the larger the shipping volume, the more attention customers will receive. Levels of attention are *high touch*, *medium touch*, and *low touch*.

High touch customers have the highest shipping volumes. Large catalog retailers and electronics firms are in this group. High volume customers are likely to seek regular competitive bidding for their delivery needs.

Medium touch customer volume is not large enough to justify a dedicated sales staff. The support carriers provide is through their call centers and the Internet. These customers are less likely to use a formal bidding process.

Low touch customers have a low shipping volume. These customers often require access to on-demand pickup services instead of daily pickup services. Customers in this group may also use retail access points. Carriers provide customer support through call centers and the Internet, and typically offer small discounts to these customers.

For shippers, there is a key issue that needs to be addressed – *is the type and volume of parcels shipped profitable for the carrier?* It is important to know what parcel characteristics, such as volume, average weight, length of haul, and percent of residential deliveries, are important to carriers. Some shippers have more profitable shipping characteristics than others. While carriers need a good mix of parcels, an understanding of what drives carriers' profitability gives shippers more leverage during the negotiation process.

1.8.3 DELIVERY SPEED

A basic consideration in parcel shipping is the *delivery speed*. Shippers often face diverse challenges as they manage outbound shipping for multiple, unrelated clients. It is the role of parcel carriers to support diverse needs by offering services based on varying levels of speed. For example, FedEx Express is a good fit for shippers with high-value or time-critical shipments and a need for fast delivery on a specific day, by a specific time. FedEx Ground is a cost-effective solution for routine shipments that do not require fast delivery. With a slower delivery time requirement the corresponding cost will be lower. The following are examples of delivery options offered by parcel carriers:

1. Same-day Airfreight is a time definite priority service to major cities when next-day delivery is not sufficient.
2. Next-day Airfreight (Overnight) is a cost-effective service that meets specific schedules by providing next-day AM or PM service to major cities.

3. Second-day or Deferred Service is a viable option when next-day delivery is not a factor. Deferred service is based on a carrier's ground delivery schedule.

Keep in mind, air service does not always mean a parcel classified as "air parcel" will travel on an airplane. Often, short-distance shipments designated as "air" will use truck service. The traditional notion of having to have an item delivered overnight, early morning is changing. The original 8 AM or 10:30 AM delivery models have expanded to included significantly lower price delivery options for noon, 3 PM, and even 5 PM next-day delivery. Deferred service, which is less expensive than traditional overnight express shipments, appeals to shippers who seek to reduce their costs, but who still require time-definite transport.

1.8.4 SHAPE AND WEIGHT

Shape and weight of an item can affect a carrier's operation in two ways: (1) shape determines equipment requirements and (2) shape and weight affect the nature of delivery. For example, a letter processed using a carrier's machinery is machinable and costs less to process than an item requiring hand processing. Manual sortation of irregular shaped and small items helps to prevent loss and damage. Carriers use a complex system of conveyor belts to sort parcels. Before shape-based pricing, USPS charged the same rate for all letters, flats, and parcels of the same weight. However, pricing based on weight alone did not accurately reflect USPS's processing and delivery cost. Processing irregular-shaped items requires more resources and lowers productivity. Using a shape-based pricing structure, in effect since May 14, 2007, USPS now considers the cost of transportation based on size, shape, and weight, *and* the different costs of processing shipments.[23] This change encourages businesses to use mailers that easily pass through USPS's automated mailing machines. Parcel carriers service four types of shipments:

Letters. Sorted on high-speed automated equipment and held by an employee when making a delivery. Letters often contain folded or flat documents but may contain other media in an envelope.

Packets. Parcels under two pounds that come in odd shapes and sizes

Parcels. Items weighing over two pounds but less than seventy pounds

Freight. Shipments over seventy pounds and may include multiple parcels sent to a single destination. Shipments handled by air typically weigh less than two hundred pounds while those shipped by ground transportation are generally heavier.

FedEx dominates the overnight letter market, but faces stiff competition from UPS and USPS. The *parcel* market is the most concentrated of the four shape-based submarkets. The difference between each carrier's focus is the average weight of "overnight" and "deferred" air parcels it handles. The average weight of parcels USPS handles is less than five pounds, while parcels delivered by its competitors typically weigh more than twice as much. UPS's success in the market for speedy transportation of parcels likely comes from its ability to pick up parcels, requiring different levels of speed, from the same shippers using an integrated pickup operation. FedEx's market share in parcel markets indicates it has a strong position in express documents.

USPS is the market leader in the delivery of air packets under two pounds. As a group, packets have physical characteristics that are the most similar to USPS's letter service. USPS also specializes in the delivery of larger parcels that require two- to three-day deferred-air service. Emery is the market leader in the overnight freight business. There are regional parcel carriers, such as Eastern Connection, that provide parcel delivery in cities from Maine to Virginia. Small by comparison to UPS and FedEx, Eastern Connection provides next-day service to many of the areas it services.

1.9 LTL Sector

While parcel carriers traditionally transport items weighing less than seventy pounds, less-than-truckload (LTL) carriers generally prefer to handle larger shipments. LTL carriers face stiff competition from the parcel sector because of the changing face of the LTL sector. As LTL carriers enter into "next-day," "overnight," and "long-haul" delivery markets, they open themselves up to competition from FedEx and UPS.[24] Because of commerce globalization and evolution of the LTL business, parcel carriers now view the LTL sector as competition. Just-in-time (JIT) delivery in manufacturing has extended into inventories and supply chains, creating a demand for smaller shipments delivered more quickly. Aware more shippers were looking for regional carriers to provide speedier service, LTL carriers began their push into the two- and three-day delivery markets. For example, YRC purchased USF Freightways, and ABF Freight System implemented its Regional Performance Model aimed at securing next-day and two-day freight.[25]

UPS and FedEx increased their share of the revenue generated by the top fifty trucking carriers from 37.5 percent in 2008 to 41.7 percent in 2009.[26] To become a force in the LTL sector, FedEx purchased regional carriers American Freightways, Viking Freight System, and Watkins Motor Lines, a long-haul LTL carrier. FedEx provides less-than-truckload freight service through its "Freight" operation (regional LTL freight services) and its "National" LTL operation (long-haul LTL freight services). To stay competitive, UPS purchased Overnight Transportation and renamed it UPS Freight. Parcel carriers and LTL carriers are similar in that they both use a network of hubs and terminals to deliver freight. However, parcel shippers tender 90 percent of manifests electronically. The opposite is true in the LTL sector, where the majority of manifests remain on paper.[27]

1.10 Parcel Consolidators

A big development in parcel shipping over the past decade has been the increased use of parcel consolidators. Parcel consolidation, also called zone skipping because parcels *skip* over some of the eight geographical zones established by the Postal Service. For example, a parcel shipped from Boston, MA, to San Diego, CA, would cross eight zones and cost the highest rate. With zone skipping, parcel consolidators and shippers with sufficient volume and weight can transport parcels direct to USPS distribution centers closer to the destination. Consolidators compete against standard parcel carriers by using a special rate from USPS called "Parcel Select."[28] USPS encourages zone skipping through its Parcel Select program. Shippers place their parcels into the postal system at one of three levels: regional bulk mailing centers (BMCs), sectional center facilities (SCFs), and destination delivery units (DDUs) or neighborhood post offices.[29] BMCs serve two to four states. SCFs serve addresses within a radius of several hundred miles and DDUs serve all or part of a town or city.

1.10.1 PARCEL SELECT RATES

Potential savings can be substantial. Shipping rates depend on the delivery zone and parcel weight. Parcels shipped through a consolidator generally cost less than a parcel carrier's average ground rate.[30] The cost to ship a parcel increases with the number of zones it passes through. For example, shipping cost for a six-pound parcel delivered to a BMC that crosses five zones will cost more than if it travels through four zones. If taken to an SCF, there is significant savings, and even more savings if deposited at a DDU. Rate tables for Parcel Select and machinable and nonmachinable mailings are available in PDF format at *www.usps.com*. To participate, Parcel Select customers must meet certain minimum weight and volume criteria, and sort parcels according to specified procedures. The high volume needed to qualify for Parcel Select rates means few shippers qualify on their own. This is where small volume shippers can benefit from the services of a parcel consolidator.

1.10.2 BRIEF HISTORY

USPS's Parcel Select program has been available since January 1999.[31] USPS has allowed drop-ship deliveries to BMCs for years, but did not allow customers to insert parcels any deeper into its system. Some companies were able to zone-skip parcels using United Parcel Service (UPS). In the late 1990s, USPS, recognizing the increasing volume of parcel shipping, encouraged consolidation. Chicago-based Donnelly and its main competitor, Quad/

Graphics subsidiary Parcel/Direct in New Berlin, Wisconsin, grew out of existing mail-oriented businesses. Their parent companies are printers of catalogs, magazines, and other direct-mail items, which give them an advantage. They have decades of experience in drop-shipping printed material into the postal system and were a natural for handling their clients' parcel business. Their ability to combine parcel traffic with shipments of printed material allows them to get the best possible rates. Large shipping volumes give giants like R.R. Donnelly and Parcel Direct a clear advantage, but they are not the only consolidators. Other consolidators include Drop Ship Express of Long Lake, Minnesota; West Coast specialist PaQFast Inc. (PFI); and Reno, Nevada-based Regional Mail Express. Following is an abbreviated timeline identifying significant developments in postal consolidation:[32]

- November 2003 – UPS and FedEx began limited testing of end delivery by USPS through UPS Basic and FedEx Last Mile.
- February 2004 – Parcel Direct acquired PaQFast.
- May 2004 – Deutsche Post Global Mail USA acquired SmartMail Services and QuikPak.
- August 2004 – Heritage Partners, principal owners of American Package Express (APX), acquired R.R. Donnelly's parcel logistics business.
- August 2004 – FedEx acquired Parcel Direct from Quad Graphics.

1.10.3 CONSOLIDATORS VERSUS. EXPEDITORS

Third-party parcel consolidators and expeditors have the volume, resources, and lower cost infrastructure to sort shipments down to the BMC and DDU levels, which enables maximum discounting. Consolidators and expeditors both perform similar functions of mixing outbound parcels, sorting them down to the BMC or DDU level, and transporting them direct to a postal hub. The key difference is a question of timing and who handles the "first mile" transportation from the shipper's dock to the service provider's facility.[33] *Consolidators* typically pick up a shipment from the shipper's facility, combine and sort it with parcels from other shippers, and transport them directly into a USPS destination facility. *Expeditors* expect clients to delivery parcels to their sortation centers. Expeditors, unlike consolidators, allow shippers to ship a trailer whenever appropriate, rather than wait for a full load to build. Consolidators and expeditors typically charge clients by adding a handling charge for each parcel shipped. Consolidators are generally less expensive, while expeditors often provide faster delivery service.

The explosive growth in online retailing, strong catalog and mail order sales, and direct marketing through television is contributing to an increase in parcel shipments. As parcel express carriers continue to raise their rates, shippers will be less willing to pay for overnight services. With the cost of overnight and priority shipping sometimes costing more than the items themselves, consumers often elect to wait an extra day or two for their order.

1.11 Electronic Commerce (E-Commerce)

Electronic commerce (e-commerce), commonly known as electronic marketing, consists of buying and selling products or services over electronic systems such as the Internet.[34] E-commerce typically uses the World Wide Web at some point in the transaction's life cycle, although it can encompass a wider range of technologies such as e-mail. Until 1991, commercial enterprise did not exist on the Internet.[35] Although the Internet became popular around 1994, it took about five years to introduce security protocols and digital subscriber lines (DSL) that allow continuous connection to the Internet. By the end of 2000, a wide range of companies offered their services through the World Wide Web. Since then, people began to associate e-commerce with the purchase of goods and services through the Internet.

1.11.1 DIFFERENTIATING B2B AND B2C[36]

Business-to-business (B2B) involves business transactions conducted electronically between two or more businesses. Electronic commerce conducted between businesses and consumers is business-to-consumer, or B2C.[37] A B2B initiative involves many participants with complex rules, higher purchasing amounts, and complex products. Unlike B2C, order fulfillment requires greater certainty. In addition, unlike B2C, brand value of a site is not critical for B2B transactions. Suppliers and buyers tend to place more importance on value-added services. Consequently, industry experts typically handle B2B e-commerce initiatives. Valuating a B2C initiative grows as the number of visitors to the site increase, but consumers gain little in the process. In a B2B initiative, the number of visitors to the site benefits buyers and sellers. With B2B, suppliers' marketing costs decrease as they find buyers more easily, even as buyers spend minimal time finding a supplier.

1.11.2 E-COMMERCE ADVANTAGES AND DRAWBACKS

E-commerce has distinct advantages over "brick and mortar" stores and mail order catalogs.[38] E-commerce offers buyers convenience. For example, consumers can search for products and services, compare prices, and buy the selected product or service without leaving their homes or offices. It is now possible for consumers to obtain a product or service, such as an electronic book, music file, or computer software, by downloading it over the Internet. For sellers, e-commerce allows them to cut costs and expand their services. They do not need to build staff, maintain a physical store, or distribute mail order catalogs. Automated order tracking and billing systems lowers labor costs; and allowing products and services to be downloaded minimizes distribution costs. There is no physical location required for products and services marketed and sold internationally. Internet technologies give sellers the ability to track the interests and preferences of customers and use the information to customize products and services to meet customer needs.

E-commerce also has drawbacks.[39] Frequently, consumers are hesitant to buy certain products online. For example, when purchasing furniture, customers often want to test its comfort before they purchase. Returning goods online involves more steps than returning an item to a store. Privacy, security, payment, identity, and contract issues arise when potential customers show concern about the privacy and security of their credit card details and what laws and jurisdictions apply.

Furthermore, the size and number of e-commerce transactions initiated online has limitations. Size directly affects the economics of transporting physical goods. While the Internet is an effective conduit for visual and auditory information—seeing pictures, hearing sounds and reading text, it does not allow full scope of one's senses. Because of the lack of sensory information, people are more comfortable buying over the Internet items they have previously seen or experienced.

1.11.3 MARKET SHARE AND PREDICTED GROWTH

In its report, titled "U.S. E-Commerce Forecast: 2008 to 2012," Forrester Research, a market research company headquartered in Cambridge, MA, predicted that online sales would reach $267.8 billion in 2010, $301 billion in 2011, and $334.7 billion in 2012.[40] Jupiter Research LLC, a research firm acquired by Forrester, forecasted lower sales in its report, "U.S. Online Retail Forecast, 2007-2012." According to Jupiter, non-travel related e-commerce sales were $128 billion in 2007, up from $108 billion in 2006. Jupiter predicted sales would grow to $182 billion in 2010, $199 billion in 2011, and $215 billion in 2012. Forrester's revenue estimate for 2008 was upward of $204 billion (a 17 percent growth rate). Instead, holiday sales in 2008 showed the first decrease in the last seven years. Because of the slowdown in online retail sales, Forrester Research issued a revised five-year forecast. Following are some stats from Forrester's revised U.S. forecast:[41]

1. E-commerce sales will represent 8 percent of all retail sales by 2014, up from 6 percent in 2009.
2. In 2009, 154 million people in the U.S. bought something online, which was 4 percent higher than in 2008.
3. Three product categories (computers, apparel, and consumer electronics) sales represented more than 44 percent of online sales in 2009.

The U.S. Census Bureau collects data in four separate surveys to measure e-commerce activity—manufacturing, merchant wholesale trade, retail trade, and selected services industries.[42] According to the latest U.S. Census Bureau's E-Stats Report, U.S. retail e-commerce sales reached almost $142 billion in 2008, up from $137 billion in 2007, an annual gain of 3.3 percent. From 2002 to 2008, retail e-sales increased at an average annual growth rate of 21.0 percent, compared with 4.0 percent for total retail sales. In 2008, e-sales were 3.6 percent of total retail sales, up from 3.4 percent in 2007. The 2008 E-Stat Report revealed that over 90 percent of retail e-sales were concentrated in two industry groups, Non-store Retailers and Motor Vehicles and Parts Dealers, which accounted for 78 percent ($111 billion) and 14 percent ($20 billion) respectively, of the sector's e-sales.

Forrester Research predicts e-commerce sales in the U.S. will keep growing at a 10 percent compounded annual growth rate through 2014. The forecast is for online domestic retail sales to approach $250 billion by 2014, up from $155 billion in 2009. While consumers purchased $155 billion worth of consumer goods online in 2009, online research influenced a far larger portion of off-line sales. Forrester estimated that $917 billion worth of retail sales in 2009 were "Web-influenced." Forrester also estimated that online and Web-influenced off-line sales would account for 53 percent of total retail sales by 2014. Each year the number of e-commerce transactions has increased and will continue to as the concept becomes more popular and natural. Work and household duties consume a significant amount of time, and the Internet affords buyers the opportunity to save time and select goods at the best price. Predictions are e-commerce will continue to grow as a major tool of sale, and rivalry within the industry will intensify its development.

1.12 Dynamics of Home Delivery[43]

E-commerce products involve home delivery. An efficient and reliable carrier delivery system is essential for gaining customer loyalty and confidence. Customers can receive some items digitally (for example, newspapers, airline tickets, and music CDs), but many products purchased online require physical transport to the end user. Home delivery refers to the delivery of goods to the customer's home (or another location of choice, such as workplace) rather than the customer going to the physical point of sale for pickup. Many other situations lead to home delivery, including delivery of traditional mail (or telephone) order products and large or heavy items such as furniture. In traditional store-based commerce, goods move from manufacturers, to wholesalers, to retailers, and finally to consumers. Retail shops function as the end of the distribution supply chain that involves a delivery carrier. See Figure 1, Product Distribution Models.

Figure 1: Product Distribution Models

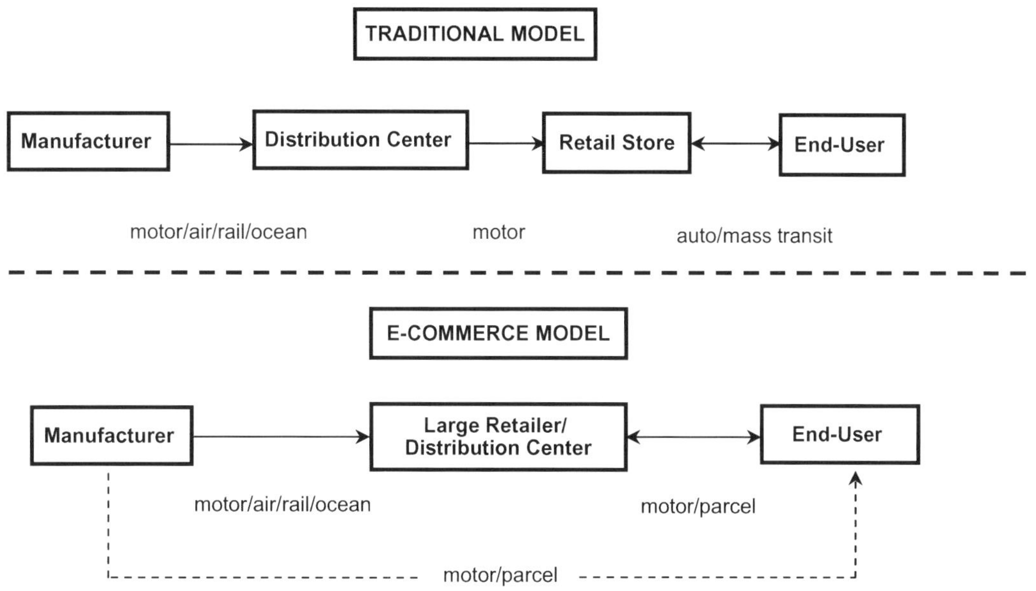

TRADITIONAL MODEL

Manufacturer → Distribution Center → Retail Store ↔ End-User

motor/air/rail/ocean — motor — auto/mass transit

E-COMMERCE MODEL

Manufacturer → Large Retailer/Distribution Center ↔ End-User

motor/air/rail/ocean — motor/parcel

motor/parcel

Source: Based on, Santish Jindel, *Delivering E-commerce,* http://www.jindel.com/Aircargoworld0399print.htm, [Online] September 2006.

Typically, customers have to take care of the "last-mile" transportation of goods, delivery from the physical point of purchase to their home. In some situations, such as a purchase of large or heavy products, the distribution supply chain may extend to customer's residence. E-commerce has changed the shape of traditional supply chains. Products purchased online move from a plant or distribution center direct to the buyer's home, regardless of shipment size. E-commerce sales generate a different transport need than the traditional delivery process. Internet technology gives buyers the ability to access manufacturers directly. The product characteristics and logistics capability of manufacturers will likely determine the growth of consumers electing to purchase over the Internet. Nonetheless, the e-commerce revolution has given buyers the ability to create a virtual just-in-time delivery system and eliminate non-value added handling and transportation costs associated with retail trade. The manufacturer to consumer e-commerce model has altered the kinds of transport seller's use. Large shipments move from manufacturers to distribution centers, and then move (as small shipments) direct to the end user, both residential and businesses.

1.12.1 IMPACT ON DELIVERY CARRIERS

Distribution of goods to retail shops involves delivery of parcel units consisting of one or more boxes, pallets, or containers filled with homogenous goods. In contrast, e-commerce delivery generally has only one item for each address and requires a different service than traditional freight transportation. The most significant impact of e-commerce on transportation is the increase in direct home delivery of smaller shipments. The extent to which e-commerce will affect transportation likely will depend on the home delivery markets and products. Smaller shipments that are more frequent become the consequence of e-commerce as manufacturers and distributors communicate directly with consumers. In addition, consumers are increasingly demanding faster delivery time and increased service quality. Table 5 presents some distinct characteristics of e-commerce delivery compared with those of traditional delivery.

Based on significant difference in the expectations of residential consignees and shipment (parcel) characteristics, the business-to-business e-commerce model has many shortcomings, which increase delivery cost when used in the business-to-residence sector:[44]

1. Generally, deliveries are early in the day when most residential customers are at work.
2. Residential areas have lower density, which increases travel time between stops.
3. Carriers pickup service is typically not user-friendly for handling returns from residential addresses.
4. Carriers equipment is designed primarily for business-to-business shipments and costly to use when delivering parcels to residences.

Key factors driving parcel carrier operations are customers' business hours, shipping patterns, information needs, and physical location. Carriers have adopted surcharges such as *residential delivery* and *proof of delivery* in an attempt to establish fee-based services and to eliminate cross-subsidies among different shipment characteristics and consignees.[45]

Table 5: Characteristics of Traditional and E-commerce Delivery

SERVICE ATTRIBUTES	TRADITIONAL DELIVERY	E-COMMERCE DELIVERY
Preferred delivery hours	8 – 12 noon	4 – 8 PM
Distribution supply chain	Producer – Wholesaler – Retailer	Online Retailer – End User
Shipment size	Large	Small
Shipment type	Homogeneous	Heterogeneous
Number of delivery stops	One or more stops	Many stops
Delivery failures	Few	Many
Delivery frequency	Low	High
Delivery time sensitivity	Low	High

Number of vehicles used	Low	High
Vehicle size	Large	Small
Delivery cost	Small	High
Claims exposure	Low	High
Weekend delivery	Infrequent	Desirable

Source: Adapted from Minyoung Park and Amelia Regan, *Issues in Emerging Home Delivery Operations*, http:www.uctc.net/scripts/countdown.pl?716pdf, accessed September 2006.

1.12.2 CARRIERS HOME DELIVERY OFFERINGS

UPS is able to spread a high volume of parcels over its network, resulting in a profitable home (parcel) delivery business. While UPS's home delivery network is large, USPS has a larger home-delivery network. Federal law requires USPS to provide delivery to every address in the U.S. every business day of the week. In contrast to UPS, USPS must provide coverage regardless of profitability. USPS delivers parcels to residences primarily through its Priority Mail product, which is predominantly a business-to-consumer (B2C) and consumer-to-consumer (C2C) product. In March 2000, FedEx launched its home delivery product to meet the needs of catalogers and online retailers.[46] The service (FedEx Ground) offers shippers and customers standard evening and Saturday delivery as well as other premium options such as day-specific pickup and delivery.

A relatively small number of carriers deliver goods purchased online to customers' homes. A fundamental premise of home delivery is to operate profitably. In order to be profitable, carriers need a sufficient density of goods for delivery within a given region. Continuing growth in e-commerce may eventually support new entrants into the home-delivery market. Companies that utilize USPS for final delivery of their products take a lower-risk approach by exposing less capital investment. However, lower risk comes at the price of lower potential margins because of the significant cost of paying USPS for final delivery. Trends show e-commerce involving quick delivery, such as grocery delivery being a slow but steady growth market. This has led to emerging delivery carriers specializing in same-day local pickup and delivery.

1.12.3 HOME DELIVERY ISSUES

The growth of e-commerce has forced online retailers and home delivery carriers to address issues related to how they organize and operate their delivery system and the service they aim to provide. One size may not fit all! A home delivery approach designed for one product may not be suitable when delivering another product. Following are some fundamental issues that arise when operating in the e-commerce environment:

No one is home. A key factor that determines the success of a home delivery operation is the availability of someone to receive the delivery. With a growing number of houses empty during the daytime and normal delivery times between 8 AM and 5 PM, difficulties are predictable. Often, there will be a need for carriers to adjust their delivery schedules to satisfy customers home delivery requirements.

Demand for faster delivery. Another critical issue for home delivery carriers is customers' demand for faster and more reliable service. While there is demand for rapid home delivery, there is little evidence that customers are willing to pay the extra cost for it. However, the trend toward faster delivery indicates express service is becoming more important in the overall mix of home delivery services. For some products, the cost of holding inventory outweighs the high cost of faster delivery service. Shortened delivery times reduce the opportunity to consolidate deliveries, resulting in higher operating costs. Carriers' ability to increase the time between ordering and delivery can improve delivery efficiency by increasing delivery density and consolidation.

Demand for reliable delivery. Demand driven by e-commerce is sensitive to time-in-transit and time-of-delivery. Increased demand for quicker and more reliable delivery service highlights the role of local delivery operations in the supply chain flow of e-commerce goods. Movement of goods locally is an important segment in the delivery process because local movement accounts for much of the overall delivery time. Redundant delivery attempts and traffic congestion affect on-time delivery and are factors to consider when planning e-commerce delivery routes and schedules. The explosive growth in e-commerce presents challenges for the parcel delivery industry. Success will depend on carriers' abilities to plan and manage their operational, pricing, and technological processes. Carriers that will benefit are those that modify their operations to handle the unique characteristics of the business-to-residence delivery market.

1.13 Wireless Information Technology

Tracking was once an activity that only occurred after a shipment failed to show up when expected. Shipping managers soon realized the value of timely and accurate information and being able to track shipments. The parcel delivery industry has a history of innovating and commercializing technologies such as bar codes, wireless computers, and electronic commerce. Carriers realized that to achieve the automation required to serve their customers more efficiently, information about a customer's shipment would have to make the transition from paper to digital. "The information about a parcel is as important as the delivery of the parcel itself," said FedEx founder Frederick Smith.[47] FedEx and UPS took the lead in capturing shipment status information and making data readily available to their customers through the Internet.

1.13.1 BAR CODE

A bar code is a series of parallel lines or bars (usually black) on a light background (usually white). The width and number of bars vary according to the bar code labeling system. The bars represent bits (binary digits) with a value of either 0 or 1. Elements (bars and spaces) in a bar code symbol must be of a consistent thickness and thinness. The first use of bar codes was to label railroad cars. Bar codes were not commercially successful until used to automate supermarket checkout systems.[48] Automated identification systems based on bar codes are a versatile technology with many applications. Systems include software and printers, as well as scanners or readers to interpret coded information. A bar code system called Universal Product Code or UPC is standard in the United States and a number of other countries.[49] Bar code technology does have limitations:

- Bar code has to be visible
- Bar code data is permanent
- Bar code takes up space on the printed item

UPS and FedEx led the curve with widespread application of bar codes and scanners to identify and track shipments, a technology now applied to individual and multi-order shipments. In 1985, FedEx became the first parcel carrier to apply a bar code to every item it processed, which helped set the modern day standard for tracking.[50] In 1993, UPS developed a two-dimensional (2D) bar code version called Maxicode specifically for auto-sortation purposes. UPS also developed an overhead optical reader for Maxicode and collaborated with Symbol Technologies Inc., to develop a handheld, wearable scanner to speed-process Maxicode-labeled packages. A one-dimensional (1D) bar code has a single row of bars. Data is encoded in the horizontal width. The 2D bar code has data encoded in both the horizontal and vertical dimensions (see Figure 2).

Figure 2: Bar code (1D and 2D) Comparison

Conventional 1D Bar code (Code 39)

2D Bar code (PDF417)

Source: Based on Wikipedia web site, Bar code samples, http://en.wiki/Bar code, accessed July 2009.

The main advantage of using a 2D bar code is that data storage capacity is significantly greater than a one-dimensional symbol. Two-dimensional symbols fall into two categories: stacked and matrix.[51] An example of "stacked" symbology is PDF417, a high-capacity bar code developed by Symbol Technologies, Inc. "PDF" which stands for Portable Data File has applications in logistics and transportation, retailing, healthcare, government, identification, and manufacturing. Examples of matrix symbologies are *DataMatrix*, *MaxiCode*, and the *QR Code*:

DataMatrix is a two-dimensional bar code that can store from one to two thousand characters. Product and serial number information are encoded on rating plates to mark surgical instruments (in Japan) and to identify items during manufacturing.

MaxiCode is a fixed-size code that holds up to ninety-three data characters. MaxiCode symbol was designed by UPS for automated scanning of parcels on high-speed conveyor lines.

The **QR Code** (Quick Response Code), developed in Japan by the Nippon Denso Company, can encode up to 2509 numeric or 1520 alphanumeric characters, and offers three levels of error detection.

Two-dimensional bar codes use similar technology as linear bar codes but carry up to one hundred times more data, and are readable even if damaged. Parcel delivery carriers use 2D symbols to encode detailed shipping information on individual parcels. Because of their advantage in low capacity applications, there continues to be a market for one-dimensional bar codes. If the application only needs a small number of characters, a 1D bar code may be the best solution.

1.13.2 RADIO FREQUENCY IDENTIFICATION (RFID)

Radio Frequency Identification (RFID) is a means of capturing data without using a human to read the data (see Figure 3). There are active and passive RFID systems. Both are comprised of three key components: tag (transponder), antenna, and reader.[52] The tag contains an intelligent agent programmed with data about the item. Readers and antennas mounted at strategic locations gather data and transmit it over radio waves to a host computer for interpretation by a software program. Antennas also transmit data to a read-write tag. Processing with an RFID is faster than with bar coded items, and it can identify multiple items simultaneously, such as individual mail trays or bags contained within a roll cage. It is also possible to read an RFID tag from any orientation.

RFID systems cost more to implement than bar code systems, but have a lower overall cost because the tags are programmable. RFID systems track hazardous materials or high-value assets using an active tag (tags with their own integrated power source). For example, INNOLOG, a logistics consultant and systems integrator based in McLean, VA, has used an RFID system to track information technology assets of the Federal Deposit Insurance Corporation (FDIC) at its facilities.[53]

Figure 3: EPC RFID Tag

Source: Based on Wikipedia web site, RFID, http://en.wikipedia.org/wiki/Radio- frequency_identification), accessed November 2006.

1.13.3 MOBILE PRINTERS

With mobile printing, parcel carriers can issue receipts, label pickups, sell postage, and collect payments. An important function provided by a mobile printer is that it gives users the ability to create a receipt with a date and time. Transaction information transmitted electronically and uploaded to a host computer system avoids manual record keeping and data entry. Route workers use mobile printers to create bar coded shipping labels for parcels picked up. Creating and applying a label in the field takes only a few seconds, but saves processing time at the company's facility. Mobile printers use cabled or wireless connectivity to receive and print documents and labels from a mobile computer or other host device. Generally, printer manufacturers offer both wireless and cable connectivity between mobile printers and their host device. Replacing cables with wireless communication reduces downtime associated with cable failure and eliminates safety risks posed by wires. Mobile printer suppliers differ on wireless options they support. The following are three widely available technologies:[54]

1. IrDA (Infrared Data Association) was the first wireless cable-replacement technology. It's use is declining rapidly, largely because of inconvenient, strict line-of-sight requirements.
2. Bluetooth wireless technology has become a top choice for replacing printer cables, especially with mobile applications that require workers to be outdoors.
3. Wi-Fi (IEEE 802.11) wireless technology is a top choice for workers "inside the four walls," especially in warehouses, manufacturing shops, hospitals, and retail establishments.

Mobile printers have proven they can increase productivity, reduce operating costs, improve cash flow, and enhance customer retention in a competitive market. The task of creating a successful mobile printing solution involves careful and thoughtful planning. For the solution to be cost-effective and applicable, it is critical to select the best print technology, media, connectivity option, and printer features. Some basic evaluation criteria that will reveal potential problems and hidden costs are ease of use, reliability, ease of integration, and customer support. As wireless technology become more available and the price of mobile printing devices decline, benefits will be difficult to ignore. A sound evaluation will determine if a particular mobile solution will deliver the productivity improvements envisioned.

1.13.4 MOBILE HANDHELD COMPUTERS

Companies whose primary business is to pick up and deliver goods achieve new levels of efficiency, productivity, and customer satisfaction when using mobile imaging systems. Drivers with handheld mobile imaging computers can capture high-quality images of parcel contents, parcel condition, signatures, bills of lading, and manifests. Wireless-enabled handheld computers also allow companies to gather customer route and accounting information right at the customer's door in real-time during pickup and delivery. This readily available information allows for faster invoicing and more accurate route planning, scheduling, and dispatching. Wireless handheld devices open direct and efficient lines of communication with customers and improve employees' working conditions. Ignoring technology can lead to inefficiencies, such as double handling of shipments.

UPS and FedEx, among the first to deploy wireless technology, rely on near-real-time data to manage operations. Wireless technologies allow carriers to capture near-real-time information in the field and in their facilities. UPS and FedEx have used various forms of wireless technology since the late 1980s, usually proprietary processes developed with vendors.[55] In recent years, both companies have switched to standards-based technologies such as 802.11b wireless LANs, Bluetooth short-range wireless links, and general packet radio service (GPRS) cellular networks.[56] UPS and FedEx have a massive scale that favors the use of global standards, which provides them more vendor choices and lower technology costs.

DIAD Handheld Computers. In 1991, UPS equipped its drivers with Delivery Information Acquisition Devices (DIADs).[57] The company has systematically added improvements to its wireless DIAD since its creation. One enhancement, Enhanced DIAD Download (EDD), is internally developed software that enables download of an electronic manifest into the driver's DIAD before he/she starts the workday. As a result, the driver can see each scheduled parcel delivery displayed on the DIAD in the order of delivery. A key EDD feature is that if a driver is about to deliver a parcel to the wrong customer, or forgets to deliver one of a group of parcels to a customer, the DIAD alerts him/her with an audible alarm. Fourth generation DIADs (DIAD IV) incorporate new radio communication links that allow them to communicate almost anywhere at any time. Expanded memory and a color screen allow color-coded alert messages.[58]

PowerPad Handheld Computer. Year 2002, FedEx and Motorola developed a handheld device to provide couriers wireless access to the FedEx network.[59] The new handheld, called PowerPad, provides parcel information to customers by allowing them to send e-mail and surf the Web from their mobile phones. PowerPad uploads scanned parcel information into FedEx's network, enabling couriers to receive real-time information and updates from any location. PowerPad's signature-capture capability enables confirmation of signature proof-of-delivery. PowerPad uses infrared connectivity to send lock and unlock signals to drop boxes its couriers visit each day, which eliminates the need to issue keys. With PowerPad, couriers no longer have to return to a van to upload parcel information or refer to manuals for shipping and service information.

Parcel carriers continue to innovate and aggressively exploit new technologies, such as automatic identification. In the process, parcel carriers have become some of the most efficient businesses in the world. In industries where distribution is a major expense and time-saving is valuable, investments in automatic identification technology can earn a strong return on investment (ROI).

1.14 Sortation Systems Technology

The challenge for parcel carriers is to reduce sorting cost. For example, FedEx's main hub in Memphis, TN, handles about two million parcels a day in a group of runways and buildings that take up about 1.5 square miles.[60] UPS's Worldport hub in Louisville, KY, has a similar scale. In their sorting facilities, both companies use a device called *ring scanner*, which is a bar code reader mounted on the employee's two fingers and wired to a terminal. As they move onto new wireless platforms, both companies are changing their approach to network security. Years before there was 802.11b standard, both UPS and FedEx had adopted predecessor wireless networks. When available, both companies immediately deployed 802.11b technology and used the maximum-security settings provided by 802.11b's wireless equivalency protocol key encryption.

Sorters and sortation systems have been designed for various applications. Cost and speed requirements and type of products handled are factors that determine the best fit. Carriers use sortation systems when moving a high flow of items to different destinations. Sortation technologies commonly accomplish the following tasks:[61]

Low Speed Sortation – Used for operations that require sort rates of less than thirty items a minute. Some examples of this technology are diverter arms, right angle transfers, pusher diverters, and work transporters.

Medium Speed Sortation – Medium rate sortation technologies provide speed rates between thirty to one hundred items. Some examples of this technology are pop-up wheel sorters and multiple belt sorters.

High-speed Sortation – High volume distribution operations require higher speed sortation devices. Critical to achieving high sortation rates are systems that properly space items before they enter the sorter. High-speed systems range from meter belts to servo-induction conveyors to multilane induction belts.

High-speed Piece Sortation – Parcel carriers sorting facilities rely heavily on this technology. Some devices used in high-speed sortation operations are carousel put systems, carousel sorters, cross belt sorters, A-frame sorters, and tilt tray sorters.

Parcel carrier operations that sort parcels by destination were some of the original users of sortation systems. These systems soon became a fixture in retail distribution centers where they break up incoming merchandise and reassemble them into new loads for outbound shipment. Sortation systems come at a price, which varies according to the complexity of the sorting application. Distribution centers that install sortation systems universally report a jump in productivity and labor utilization. In addition, sortation systems often make it possible for companies to take advantage of "zone-skipping" programs, which can lower parcel-shipping cost.[62]

1.15 Global Environment

Globalization is an important characteristic within the economic environment. Globalization has resulted in significant change to economic development for many countries. The drive for globalization has resulted in greater economic growth globally, through lowering barriers to international trade. Over recent decades, the breaking down of economic barriers between nations has resulted in greater worldwide economic growth. When FedEx helped introduce air-express service some thirty years ago, the idea of a global economy that was interdependent and integrated was largely theoretical. Now cross-border manufacturing has become an environmental trend. Estimates are that 20 percent of manufactured goods are consumed cross international borders.[63] In cross-border manufacturing, streamlining supply chains to ensure the efficient flow of physical goods and information and controlling cost are paramount concerns. Cross-border manufacturing and global sourcing activities have created a strong demand for fast and efficient transportation services. With the global economy's increasing reliance on trade, countries are increasingly dependent on efficient and competitive means of exporting and importing goods from other countries. Following are some aspects to global transport service that are important to shippers:[64]

Speed. For some businesses, speed to market is often more important than transportation costs, in determining their competitiveness. An example is perishable goods such as pharmaceutical test material.

Reliability. Failure to make deliveries on time can jeopardized a company's reputation.

Destination served. Globalization and global purchasing by companies means the ability to ship products to and from an increasing number of countries cost-effectively and quickly is important.

Government restrictions and complex policies undermine the ability of companies to operate efficiently in the global environment. Anticompetitive practices involve subsidizing monopolies, imposing special taxes on foreign competitors, complex licensing requirements, inefficient customs procedures, restrictions on access to aviation markets, restrictions on foreign investments, or the outright exclusion of competition. Complex and restrictive policies hinder competition across the global economy and place an economic burden on companies doing business globally.

1.15.1 GLOBAL SHIPPING COMPLEXITIES

From a shipper's perspective, globalization means more volume and longer lead-time for its shipments. An attraction of the Internet is the potential to tap into a vast global market. However, shippers need to be aware of the complexities associated with global shipping. Shippers have grown accustomed to the convenience of services offered by parcel carriers, and often take them for granted. Shipping to off-the-beaten-path destinations may seem simple, but the cost may exceed value of the product. For shippers to succeed in the global marketplace, they have to acquire specialized knowledge associated with global shipping. Major parcel carriers have made it easier than ever to navigate the logistics and regulations associated with global shipping. Getting the product to its destination on time and in one piece is the ultimate responsibility of the shipper. Following are examples of the complexities shippers face when shipping globally:[65]

Classifying products using commodity codes based on universal standards. Codes referred to as harmonized codes or schedule B codes describe goods in trade.

Checking *the product* to ensure it complies with U.S. and the destination country's import and export regulations.

Identifying U.S. government licensing requirements and applicable license exceptions based on the product's Export Control Classification Number.

Conducting research to ensure the consignee is not on a denied party list, called a "Restricted Party Screening."

Submitting required documents, such as a Shipper's Export Declaration (SED). To comply with U.S. regulations, filing an SED electronically with the Department of Census' Automated Export System (AES) is required.

Informing the customer on how much the shipment is going to cost. Cost will include customs fees, duties or taxes, brokerage, and other charges involved in customs clearance.

1.15.2 GLOBAL AIRFREIGHT SERVICE

Air Cargo Management Group (ACMG) reported that revenue for the U.S. domestic airfreight and express industry totaled $31.88 billion in 2008.[66] ACMG also reported the U.S. domestic airfreight and express industry continues to be dominated by express carriers. This group, led by FedEx and UPS, had a 67.5 percent market share (in ton-mile terms) in 2008. The airfreight business requires complex support networks and business acumen. Being an airfreight carrier often means having distribution centers, offices, and hubs located close to markets. It requires an integration of hardware with Web-based networks. These requirements have become standard for both integrated carriers and freight forwarders. For example, UPS is an integrated airfreight carrier that operates worldwide. UPS's business direction is the result of several strategic decisions by UPS, including building a global network, investing in technology, and acquiring companies with freight operations and expertise.[67] Express carriers recognize global shipping is where the growth is, and have set it as a high priority in their own growth. Revenue from FedEx's international priority service represented 26 percent of the company's 2008 revenue, up from 17 percent eight years earlier.[68] International small package shipping generated 22 percent of UPS's revenue in 2008, or $11.29 billion.[69]

Experts predict that China will become the world's second-largest economy by 2016 and the largest by 2039. According to Armand Zrreza, administrator of the Subic Bay Metropolitan Authority, China is larger than the entire market of Southeast Asia. For UPS, the goal is to offer domestic express parcel service across much of China. Today, China is one of the fastest growing markets in DHL's global network.

1.15.3 NAVIGATING THE GLOBAL MARKETPLACE

Shippers have come to rely on parcel carriers not just to provide transportation but also to manage the complexities of international shipping. In today's environment, shippers expect carriers to provide a comprehensive custom service, which includes automated clearance, reporting, and drawback claims. Carriers provide international trade software that allows shippers to track their goods and ensure compliance with export regulations. Parcel carriers also have developed Web-based tools that guide their customers through the global shipping process.[70]

UPS developed its "TradeAbility" software package to assist shippers overcome international trade obstacles. The software helps shippers generate cost estimates for duties, taxes, and transportation and find compliance information for foreign countries. UPS's "WorldShip" software provides direct Internet connection between shippers' databases and UPS's air and ground information systems. *FedEx* has focused on developing technology that improves the speed and reliability of its global express services. Among the tools available to shippers is FedEx "InSight," a Web-based program that provides visibility into inbound, outbound, and third-party shipments. This program allows shippers to find out about customs-clearance delays while it is still early enough to take corrective action. FedEx's "Global Trade Manager" service, which includes import and export documents from more than two hundred countries, assists in inland transport cost calculations and conducts denied-party screening for exports. DHL offers global shipping tools, such as "EasyShip" software, for shippers of all sizes. In addition, DHL offers "Import Express Online," which helps importers prepare import shipments and manage shipping details from pickup to delivery.

Economists consider FedEx and UPS to be bellwethers of the global economy since they deal with product shipments, which is a basic indicator of economic health. Slowing down of the global economy has affected their financial performance. Consumers are buying less; therefore businesses are spending less on shipping. West Coast airports that had been the beneficiaries of a booming trade relationship with Asia are feeling the pinch of the 2008 recession. Despite gaining new customers, as the result of DHL's withdrawal from the U.S. domestic market, UPS and FedEx continue to prepare for the global economy to rebound.

SECTION II — GENERAL PACKAGING GUIDELINES

2.0   Container (or Package) Type

2.1   Load Types

2.2   Package Acceptability

2.3   Elements of Packaging

2.4   Protecting Perishables

2.5   Hazardous Materials

2.6   Export Packaging

2.7   Shipping Containers

2.8   Corrugated Boxes

2.9   Other Shipping Containers

2.10 ESD-Protective Packaging

2.11 Pre-shipment Container Testing

2.12 Vendor Packaging Compliance

SECTION II

GENERAL PACKAGING GUIDELINES

THE DIVERSITY AND DISPARITY of goods transported make it nearly impossible to write a packaging guideline for each commodity. To deliver parcels on time and damage free, two critical steps need to take place. One, the shipper must give the carrier a properly packaged product, and second, the carrier must handle the product properly. Minimizing shipping damage begins long before parcels ever reach the carrier. Safe and on-time delivery begins with careful packaging preparation. In the carrier delivery environment, carriers such as USPS, UPS, and FedEx transport parcels. In this environment, automated equipment plays a dominant role in parcel processing. This involves the "hand-to-surface" method, where parcels move from truck to conveyor belt to truck, and the varying conditions of transport. Parcels change hands many times from pickup to delivery, which increases the likelihood they will fall or contact other parcels.

Parcel (or express) carriers have basic packaging guidelines, which establish minimum and maximum allowable shape, size, and weight. Carriers also have Terms and Conditions (T&Cs), which establish shipping guidelines. It is the shipper's responsibility to determine if shipments meet carriers' T&Cs. Many carriers' websites allow access to their rules and various shipping functions, such as scheduling a pick up and tracking a shipment:

- Emery Forwarding – www.emeryworldwide.com
- FedEx – www.fedex.com
- UPS – www.ups.com
- U.S. Postal Service – www.usps.com

2.0 Container (or Package) Types

Type 1, Type 2, and Type 3 are the Institute of Professional Packagers container (or package) design recommendations:[71]

Type 1 – factory packed, pre-engineered, custom container design dedicated to one product. This includes a product in the center of container unless its fragility differs by orientation, or it is critical to move the container's center of gravity. Shipping containers used will depend largely on the method of packing, shape, and orientation of container contents. Container strength and interior protective packaging should be cost-effective and consistent with product protection, packing labor, and customer requirements. For high value products, use a higher strength and product protection level than used for moderate and lower value products. Establishing a benchmark of percentage cost of packaging to total product-manufacturing cost will help determine if packaging costs are equitable within a product line.

Type 2 – miscellaneous items packed in random order at fulfillment centers, catalog houses, and pick and pack operations. This includes one or more items packed together in a shipping container of adequate size. Many companies have developed packaging guidelines that define relative product fragility and the amount and thickness of protective packaging required. Items deemed fragile should have more clearance from container walls and more separation from other items in the container. Container contents should not weigh more than 50 percent of the maximum allowable weight listed on the box manufacturer's certificate (BMC). Containers should be of sufficient strength to maintain required clearance between contents and all six-container walls (top, bottom, and four sides). Often, the environmental impact of packaging material is an important issue for customers. Customers may require the same material for containers and interior packaging for commingling by recyclers.

Type 3 – occasional packaging of miscellaneous items. This includes containers prepared infrequently by factories, warehouses, mailing stores, or individuals. The container contents vary and may be any item accepted for shipment. Because these items ship infrequently and in low volume, environmental impact and related issues are of little concern. Fragility, while important, is not always easily determined. Therefore, the most important factor in determining packaging becomes the intrinsic value of the item. High value items require stronger containers with more cushioning protection than average value items. Contents of corrugated containers should not exceed 50 percent of allowable gross weight as printed on the box manufacturer's certificate (BMC). A general rule is at least three inches of cushioning material on all six sides of the item.

2.1 Load Types

In the transportation industry, the term *load* defines a quantity of material assembled and packaged as a shipping unit.[72] Generally, package classification depends on the contents, how well the packaging protects it, and the strength of the shipping container.

Easy loads include moderate-density items packed in interior receptacle containers. Shock, compression, or puncture does not have an extreme effect on easy loads during shipping. This type load does not shift or move within the container and usually does not endanger other parcels.

Average loads include moderately concentrated items that usually provide partial support to all surfaces of the shipping container. Compression is a hazard that can affect average loads during transport. Average loads can ship directly in a container or in separate interior containers. Nesting items within partitions or separate paperboard boxes can stabilize an average load and prevent damage to the container.

The items in *difficult loads* usually need additional protection against shock, puncture, or distortion during handling and shipping. Fragile objects, delicate instruments, high-density items, and small bulk items are difficult loads. Paper boxes, paper or plastic bags, or wraps cannot support difficult loads and are not acceptable containers.

2.2 Package Acceptability

Carriers will apply their container acceptability standards to determine if they will accept a container for shipment.[73] Avoid packing containers in a manner that could cause bodily injury to employees or damage other containers and equipment. Pack fragile items to withstand processing and transporting. Brace and cushion heavy items to prevent damage to other containers. Items described below can cause problems if packaged improperly. The United States Postal Service *Domestic Mail Manual* provides detailed packaging guidelines.[74]

2.2.1 STATIONARY

These items frequently become loose during shipping. Frequently, problems occur because of unrestrained, concentrated, or shifting contents resulting from inadequate internal packaging, containers, closures, and reinforcements. Band stationary items together or use partitioning containers to prevent shifting. Letter-style envelopes are not adequate for mailing items thicker than one inch or heavier than one pound.

2.2.2 LIQUIDS

Improperly packaged liquids can cause injury and damage processing equipment and other containers. Generally, containers of liquid with only friction-top closures (pushdown type) are not acceptable. Screw-on caps, soldered tops, clips, or other means are necessary for a secure closure. It is best to cushion glass and other breakable containers holding more than four fluid ounces with a material that can readily absorb leakage. To be acceptable cushion a container and pack it within another sealed, leak-proof container, such as a can or plastic bag. The outer container should be strong enough to protect the contents and be marked "LIQUID." Containers should display orientation markings such as, "UP ARROWS" that indicate the upright position of the parcel. Shippers should consult Department of Transportation (DOT) and Performance Oriented Packaging (POP) mandates to ensure shipments of liquid hazardous materials meet Federal regulations.

2.2.3 AEROSOLS

Aerosol containers that have an inadequate friction-cap or other means to prevent accidental discharge of contents can cause injury or damage to other containers and processing equipment. It is important to use a container that is constructed to prevent accidental discharge of its contents.

2.3 Elements of Packaging

Many items require proper containment before they ship from one place to another. To function successfully, containers must adequately hold the product. Today, packaging production is more efficient than ever before. Packaging has evolved from a small range of heavy, rigid containers made of wood, glass, and steel to a broad array of rigid, semi-rigid, and flexible packaging made from specialized lightweight materials. The four basic elements of packaging are: (1) exterior packaging, (2) cushioning, (3) closure, sealing, and reinforcing, and (4) marking and labeling.

2.3.1 EXTERIOR PACKAGING[75]

Corrugated Box. This type of container provides the best protection and is the ideal way to ship most items. The box should be in good, rigid condition with all flaps intact. Corrugated boxes lose a degree of their original protective properties during each use. Boxes that have punctures, tears, rips, or corner damage may not adequately protect the item. Double-wall corrugated boxes provide enhanced strength, which make them suitable for transporting heavy items. Boxes should be large enough to allow room for adequate cushioning on all sides of the item (see Appendix 3, Exterior Packaging Materials).

Original Manufacturers Packaging. Generally, the original manufacturer's packaging is for shipments on pallets instead of single piece consignments. The reuse of original packaging to send an item through a parcel delivery network increases risk of product damage. Only use a manufacturer's box by itself if it is in new condition and can withstand impact.

Double Boxing. This choice makes use of the original manufacturer's packaging. Inspect the container to insure the original packaging is in good condition. Replace broken foam inserts with new inserts or repair damaged inserts using pressure-sensitive tape. Fill the bottom of a new shipping container with a cushioning material, such as foam-in-place, loose-fill peanuts, or other suitable dunnage material. Place original manufacturer's box on top of cushioning material and in the center of the shipping container. Apply cushioning around the remaining five sides of the manufacturer's box. Seal shipping container with pressure-sensitive, nylon-reinforced, or water-activated reinforced tape. To seal the outer box, close the box and apply tape to its top and bottom.

Padded Bags. A protective bag is the recommended method for shipping items such as books, diskettes, and videos. For added strength, the inside of a lightweight bag is lined with bubble film to absorb any impact. Padded bags can be inserted into a Link Letter or City Pack bag for added security and protection.

2.3.2 CUSHIONING

It is important to cushion or pad the contents of a container. A properly prepared container for shipment uses cushioning. Cushioning materials serve one or more of the following functions:[76]

- Fills voids and cushions contents from shock and vibration
- Braces or blocks to eliminate movement
- Protects contents from abrasion, corrosion, temperature extremes, and ESD (electrostatic discharge)

The type, weight, and sensitivity of the goods shipped determine what cushioning material to use. The padding should be suitable to protect goods during transport and not allow contact between the goods and outer packaging. Wrap items separately and leave clearance around the corners and sides of the box. The recommendation is to leave at least two-inches of space between the outer container and the item. Fill space with an internal protection material of some type. Following are some common cushioning methods:[77]

Blocking and Bracing. By using a resilient material, shippers can block and brace their shipments. The material will absorb the shock energy and direct it toward the strongest point of the product. Blocking and bracing is the preferred cushioning method for heavyweight containers.

Flotation. Flotation (sometimes called *stuffing*) is a method of surrounding an object with small pieces of cushioning material that shifts or flows to fill empty space in a container. This method distributes impact over the entire surface of an object and works best when combined with other packaging methods.

Wrapping. This method uses sheet material of various types to wrap small items individually. This method does not provide adequate protection for heavy items.

Suspension. This method keeps packaged items away from the sides of the container. Materials used for suspension are straps, tape, slings, polyfilm, and other supports that function as flexible restraints.

Mold Enclosures. Molded enclosures distribute forces and conform to the contour of item.

Examples of cushioning or internal packaging materials include foamed plastics, rubberized hair, corrugated fiberboard, and loose-fill materials such as excelsior, polystyrene, and shredded newspapers. Combinations of several types of cushioning, such as corrugated fiberboard pads and loose-fill material, help dissipate shock and pressure. The following are materials commonly used to cushion items:

Polyethylene Bubble Wrap. This material is comprised of pockets of air distributed on plastic film, designed to protect and cushion lightweight items from shock, vibration, and abrasion.

Polyethylene Foam. This is a soft nonabrasive and lightweight cushioning material used for wrapping delicate items.

Inflatable Packaging (Air Bags). This is a cushioning material used primarily as void-fill material for lightweight items. This material is not suitable for use with items having sharp corners or edges.

Loose Fill Expanded Polystyrene (Peanuts). This is used as a void fill material for lightweight items. This material is not used with flat or narrow products that may move to the edge or bottom of container during transit. Because of the shifting and settling properties of peanuts, place a minimum of three inches of cushioning around the contents.

Engineered Foam Enclosures. Enclosure materials include expanded polystyrene, polyethylene, polypropylene, or copolymers, pre-engineered for specific products.

Foam-in-Place. This material is a chemical mixture that expands and forms a protective mold around container contents.

Crumpled Kraft Wrapping Paper or Newspaper. This is used primarily as a void-fill material for light- to medium-weight non-fragile items.

Corrugated Paper Rolls and Inserts. These are materials added to a container to increase its strength and improve its performance.

Cushion Wrap. Single-faced corrugated paper is ideal for packing items such as, books, CDs, and videos.

NOTE: Slightly overfilling a container's interior with cushioning material will help hold items in place and prevent movement.

2.3.3 CLOSURE, SEALING, AND REINFORCING[78]

Closing, sealing, and reinforcing are prime considerations in preparing a container for shipment.

Closure methods suited to ship palletized boxes may be inadequate for individual shipments. Higher grades of closure material will help protect items from stress levels frequently encountered by single shipments. Standard methods of box closure include adhesives and glues, banding and strapping, staples and steel stitching, and taping (pressure-sensitive and gummed). Avoid masking or cellophane tapes because they do not provide the strength necessary for proper container sealing. Also, avoid using strings or cords because these items can catch on automated processing equipment. Single strip tape closure is normally acceptable when using a premium grade pressure-sensitive tape or premium reinforced gummed-paper tape. For a durable closure, when using low-grade tape, place strips of tape at right angles across the flap joints at the end of the box (six-strip or H method). Containers weighing over sixty pounds may require reinforcement with bands of nonmetallic strapping or reinforced tape (see Appendix 4, Comparative Securing Systems).

Adhesives. These products are made from synthetic materials, such as resins, that stick to the surface of other substances and bond them together. *Glue* is a form of adhesive made from natural materials.[79] Some common applications for glue are sizing paper and textiles, labeling, sealing, and manufacturing paper goods. Some synthetic adhesives, such as epoxy resins, are strong enough for construction purposes. Consider the following issues before selecting an adhesive:[80]

- What is the objective?
- Under what conditions does it need to stick?

- How quick must the adhesive be at full strength?
- How strong must the adhesive be?
- What properties, such as clear or sandable, must it have when dry?

An adhesive used to close a container is adequate if at least a 50-percent fiber tear occurs on the box flap surface after opening the container. An adhesive used on tapes or box flaps should remain serviceable in temperatures from -20° to 160° Fahrenheit. When used on box flaps, adhesive should cover more than 50 percent of the box flaps and be applied no more than one-quarter inch from the box flap ends. As an alternative, apply four strips of hot-melt adhesive on each part of the box flap where the outer flap lies over the inner flap. To use this method, adhesive strips must have the following characteristics: (1) be three-sixteenths of an inch wide after compression, (2) be no more than one and a half inches apart with the first strip no more than half an inch from the center seam, and (3) be extended to full width of the inner flap (Figure 4 illustrates placement of box flap adhesive).

Figure 4: Box Flap Adhesive

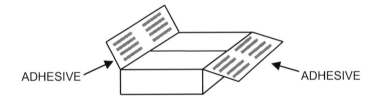

Bandings (or strapping). This method uses metallic and nonmetallic banding and pressure-sensitive filament tape to secure a container. Flat steel banding should have smooth or plastic-coated edges, and banding ends covered or protected. When using banding to close and reinforce a container, at least one band must encircle the length and a second band must encircle the girth, as shown in Figure 5. Loose strapping, especially metal, is not acceptable because it does not reinforce the container and constitutes a danger to carrier employees and parcel-processing equipment. Bands should be tight enough to depress the box corners. Specific banding material and the grade best suited for packaging depends on factors such as shape and weight of the container, method of shipment, and shipping distance. Banding is for delicate bundling, whereas strapping is for shipping boxes and other heavy-duty applications.

Figure 5: Banding (or strapping)

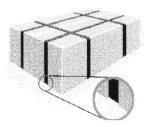

Source: Adapted from United States Postal Service, Domestic Mail Manual (DMM), Publication 2 (January 2002), Packaging for Mailing, Section 4 – Closing Sealing and Reinforcing

Plastic strapping compared to steel strapping is less expensive, lighter weight, and laborsaving because it is easier to apply.[81] Plastic strapping is flexible and tensioning stretches the strap. A built-in memory characteristic allows it to recover initial strength as a load settles or becomes compressed by top weighting or stacking. Plastic straps can absorb shock and will not easily snap or break. They are easy to remove without the "backlash" often associated with a steel strap.

Staples and Steel Stitching. Staples and stitching are acceptable for closing a container when applied not more than five inches apart for an easy or average load and not more than two and a half inches apart for a difficult load. The number of staples required depends on factors such as corrugated board quality, container contents, and type staples. Figure 6 illustrates some common stapling methods.

Figure 6: Staple Closure Methods

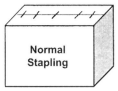 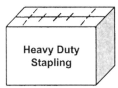

Place staples not more than one and a quarter inches from the ends of the shipping container. When not possible to meet staple spacing requirements, band the box to compensate

for any gap in the staple closure. An alternative would be to apply a strip of three-inch wide reinforced tape to the container between staples. Some features and benefits of stapling are (1) lower costs, (2) strength and security (3) attractive and pilfer-proof, and (4) environmentally friendly.[82]

1. Lower costs. Simplified packaging design and less material is used when staples are the closing method.
2. Strength and security. Stapling is ideal for packaging heavy items for long-distance transport. Staples maintain well in all weather (damp, dusty, hot, or cold) and environmental conditions.
3. Attractive and pilfer-proof. Staples leave a clear and unmarred surface and are a deterrent to theft.
4. Environmentally friendly and efficient. Staples are 100 percent natural and easily recyclable. In addition, they only require one-fortieth of the space used by tape.

Taping. Tapes used to close, seal, and reinforce shipping containers are fundamental to shipping. The use of gummed tape provides a better bond between the tape and box surface. The liquid glue penetrates deep into the fibers of the box surface. The adhesive strip holds even when exposed to environmental conditions such as extreme temperatures, dust, long storage, and moisture. Self-adhesive tapes are easy to apply and are an alternative for normal application.

Pressure-sensitive tape, also known as PSA tape, adhesive tape, self-stick tape, or sticky tape, was first developed in 1845 by Dr. Horace Day, a surgeon.[83] Pressure-sensitive tape will stick without the need for solvent, heat, or water activation. By contrast, a "gummed" or "water-activated" adhesive tape requires warm water for activation. Tape used to close and reinforce shipping containers should not be less than two inches wide. Pressure-sensitive tape works best when applied to clean surfaces at temperatures above freezing. Cellophane and masking tapes are not adequate for closing or reinforcing containers, but can supplement an adhesive closure on items such as, envelopes.

Gummed tape is acceptable for closing and reinforcing shipping containers when using water to activate the adhesive. If not properly activated, the container will absorb the water and the gummed tape will not stick to the container. Tape applied correctly will remain attached to the container during handling. Removal of the tape will cause separation or at least a 50-percent fiber tear on taped surfaces. Tape should be kept away from freezing temperatures for at least one hour before applying. Even properly applied gummed tape can crack in extremely cold temperatures. Two commonly used gummed tapes are reinforced paper (Kraft) and non-reinforced paper (Kraft).

Reinforced paper (Kraft) tape is acceptable for closing irregular-shaped or soft-wrapped containers. A shipping container closed with reinforced paper tape is more durable than one that uses non-reinforced paper tape.

Non-reinforced paper (Kraft) tape is acceptable for closing shipping containers if the tape is rated at a minimum sixty-pound weight basis. Tape should extend at least two and a half to three inches over the adjoining side of the container.

Using an H-seal (six-strip) versus a Center Seam for Closure. Box closure is important for single shipments. Higher grades of closure materials are often required. The standard use of box closure and sealing tape for a regular slotted container (RSC) is a center seam or single strip closure.[84] Placing a strip of tape along the center seam of a box, extending about two and a half to three 3 inches onto the ends of the box will seal it adequately. An H-seal closure can provide additional security for a "difficult" container. The H-seal closure method will use more tape, and require more labor for application. The H-seal method is not suited for automated processing equipment. Figure 7 illustrates center seam and H-seal box closure methods.

Figure 7: Center Seam and H-seal Box Closure Methods

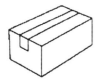 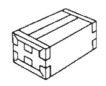

Center Seam or Single Strip closure   H-seal (six strip closure)

Source: Based on illustrations presented in *Canadian Department of Foreign Affairs and International Trade* publication, "Export Packaging," Third Edition by The Mariport Group LTD., Burlington, Ontario, 2000.

2.3.4 MARKING AND LABELING

It is important to mark and label shipping containers with routing information to include delivery and return addresses. The information must be legible and easily understood. Place a return address in the upper left corner of container or address label (see Figure 8). Include inside the container the name and address of the shipper and recipient, and a description of the enclosed contents. Generally, carriers do not require exterior markings that identify the contents of a container. The following labeling tips will help ensure efficient handling and on-time delivery:[85]

Correct Placement. Place the shipping label on top of the container and a packing slip on the same surface.

Incorrect Placement. Do not place a label over a seam, closure, or on top of sealing tape.

Visibility. Avoid placing tape or film over the label.

Label Condition. Avoid wrinkles, tears, stains, or stray marks. Do not mark on the borders. Remove or cross out old labels and markings on a used box.

Odd-shaped Containers. Place label on the largest side of an irregularly shaped container. Do not wrap labels around a handle or cylinder to cause the edges to overlap.

Addresses. Include the recipient's postal code, suite, or apartment number with the complete street address. In addition, place delivery information inside the container and include a return address.

P.O. Box Address. Attempt to obtain a street address before using a P.O. Box address. If it is necessary to use a P.O. Box address, contact the carrier ahead of time to ensure it delivers to P.O. Boxes, Army Post offices (APO), and Fleet Post Office (FPO) addresses.

Information provided on a label can mean the difference between a parcel delivered on time and one delayed, or lost. The use of barcoding has become universal, and can be found in the shipping industry in the form of "smart labels."[86] The smart label is a computer-generated shipping label. A key element of the smart label is the barcode. Smart labels increase shipping reliability and improve transit time. Proper placement of a shipping label is on the top flaps of the shipping container. A coded system that identifies container contents helps to reduce theft or pilferage of valuable items. Place a label or marking on two surfaces of the shipping container if container contents require a warning such as *Electromagnetic* or *ESD sensitive*.

Figure 8: Addressing Your Parcel

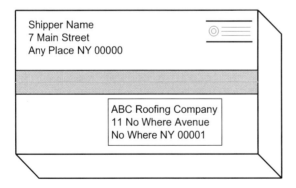

NOTE: <u>Delivery Address</u> should be printed or typed parallel to the longest side of the parcel. <u>Return Address</u> should be printed or typed in the upper left corner on the front of the parcel. Commas and periods should be omitted.

Source: Based on USPS web site, accessed December 2009, http://www.usps.com/send/images/letter.jpg.

Markings and Symbols. Specialized markings for shipping containers have been around for years. Items transported with special markings give personnel who are handling, moving, or storing the items precautionary warnings and special handling instructions. For example, hazardous material shipments require specified markings, as set forth in the Code of Federal Regulations (CFR), Title 49. Additional markings are in Item 682 of the National Motor Freight Classification (NMFC), titled "Pictorial Precautionary Markings." Shippers should consult "Pictorial Markings for the Handling of Goods," published by ASTM (D5445), ISO (780), and carrier rules, if their container requires special handling considerations, such as FRAGILE, PERISHABLE, DO NOT BEND. Remove obsolete markings on reused boxes and other containers and apply new markings with a waterproof material.

2.4 Protecting Perishables

A shipment is a perishable if its contents *deteriorate over a given period if exposed to harsh environmental conditions, such as excessive temperature or humidity.*[87] The United States Department of Transportation (DOT) and the International Air Transport Association's (IATA) rules govern perishable shipments. Shippers of perishable commodities should consult their carriers regarding applicable carrier rules. Perishable products include fruits, vegetables, meats, dairy products, horticultural products (flower bulbs and ornamentals) and certain chemicals, photographic supplies, and pharmaceuticals. Many products are sensitive to temperature change. In fact, with some chemical products, a chemical reaction can occur if temperatures fall outside a specified range. Understanding a product's temperature requirement is critical to ensure it arrives at its destination in good condition. Shippers of perishable products should consider three key factors: insulation, refrigerants, and protective packaging.

2.4.1 INSULATION

Insulation is any material that prevents or reduces the transfer of heat. The objective of insulation is to keep commodities refrigerated, frozen, or warm, or to reduce the effects of extreme temperature variations.[88] The unit of measure for insulation properties is thermal conductivity, or K-factor. K-factor is a rate at which heat flows through a material or insulation. The lower the K-factor, the better the insulation value of the material. R-factor is the measure of resistance to heat flow. R-value is the reciprocal (1/K) of K-factor. A high R-value indicates good insulation. With "everything being equal," as the thickness of the insulation increases, resistance to heat flow increases. Some traditional insulation materials are expanded polystyrene foam (EPS), rigid high-density polyurethane (spray-in-place foam), and reflecting surface material (radiant barrier film).

The vacuum insulation panel (VIP) is a technologically advanced product that combines high R-value in a relatively thin panel.[89] VIPs consist of a filler material, or core, encapsulated by a thin, barrier material, such as metal foil, to hold a vacuum for long periods. The core not only provides the structural integrity of the VIP, but also prevents heat transmission through the VIP. Often, with smaller shipping containers, much of the volume is insulation. Keeping the internal volume of a container constant allows reduction of the outer dimension (Figure 9 illustrates this concept). This reduces heat loss and gain and allows for a reduction in phase change material, such as dry ice and gel packs. For temperature-controlled packaging, advantages include greater thermal control, improved energy efficiency, more internal space, reduced packaging size, extended shipping time, lower weight, and lower shipping costs.

Figure 9: Tradition Insulating Materials vs. Equivalent VIP

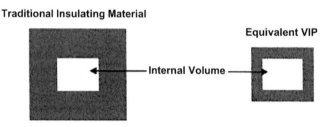

NOTE: VIP's provide an insulating capability far greater than an equivalent thickness of traditional insulation material.

Researchers at Berkeley Environmental Energy Technologies Division developed a gas-filled panel made of honeycombed layers of thin aluminized plastic filled with a gas such as argon, krypton, or xenon. Cargo Technology, Inc., based in San Diego, CA, licensed this advanced insulating material for use as thermal packaging for perishable shipments. Cargo's product, *AirLiner*, is an inflatable, insulating bag that converts an ordinary corrugated box into a cooler to keep perishables cold during shipping.[90] Expanded polystyrene foam containers, a thirty-year old technology, prone to cracking and leaking, is the choice of many to keep perishables cold.

2.4.2 REFRIGERANTS

Refrigerant (coolant) products control the internal temperature of a container. Refrigerants are the lowest cost component of the container. Refrigerants can maintain three temperature ranges: refrigerated, frozen, and warm.[91] The temperature requirement of the perishable determines the required refrigerant. Some common types of refrigerants are dry ice, refrigerant packs (gel, foam), and wet ice. The most popular is "gelletized" water, often referred to as a "gel pack." Gel packs cannot reach the temperature that dry ice can, nor does gelletized ice absorb as many BTUs per pound as dry ice. However, gel packs are reusable, inexpensive, and do not give off gas during the thawing process. Wet ice has disadvantages, including weight, tendency to thaw or leak, and they require water resistance packaging. Conduct tests to determine refrigerants required to meet a particular need. The following are concerns to address when shipping temperature-sensitive products:[92]

1. Will shipments go to the same customer, or single shipments to many customers, or a combination of the two?
2. Where are the customers located?
3. What is the expected time-in-transit for shipping the product?
4. Does the product require overnight shipping, early morning delivery, or can it travel for three to five days or longer?

Dry ice is a solid form of carbon dioxide that has a surface temperature of -109° F (-78° C). A beneficial characteristic of dry ice is that it changes from liquid to gas during the thawing process, which gives "dry ice" its name.[93] Dry ice does not have a liquid state and will not saturate the container with water. Shippers use dry ice when transporting frozen and perishable products, such as meat, poultry, fish, and ice cream. Governing regulations are the biggest drawback to using dry ice. The DOT and IATA set federal rules that govern shipping dry ice. Dry ice is a "miscellaneous" hazard, Class 9, and considered hazardous during transport for the following reasons:[94]

1. Explosion hazard: Dry ice releases carbon dioxide gas as it sublimates. If placed in a container that does not allow release of the gas, it could explode, causing personal injury or property damage.
2. Suffocation hazard: A large volume of carbon dioxide gas emitted in a confined space may displace oxygen and create an oxygen deficient environment.
3. Contact hazard: Dry ice is a cryogenic material that can cause severe frostbite upon contact with skin.

Do not use dry ice with materials that can become brittle or permeable. There are commercial packaging systems specifically designed for shipping dry ice. Never place dry ice in a container with an airtight seal and use appropriate markings and labels when transporting a commodity by air and water, or through a parcel carrier.[95] IATA limits dry ice in each container to 200 kg. DOT and IATA require shippers to list the net weight of dry ice in kilograms. Dry ice labels and markings (see Figure 10) are required along with hazardous material labels and markings.

Figure 10: Class 9, Dry Ice Label and Markings

Carbon dioxide, solid
(Dry Ice)
UN1845
_____ kg.

NOTE: Class 9 label satisfies DOT and IATA marking labeling requirements when completed accurately.

Source: Adapted from Federal Motor Carrier Safety Administratin web site, Part 179.446: Class 9 label, http://www.fmcsz.dot.gov/rules-regulations/administration/fmcsr/fmcsrruletext, aspx, accessed December 2009

Use two millimeter or thicker watertight plastic bags and double bag perishable products that contain liquid or may thaw. Permitted is a lined EPS container with a two millimeter or thicker plastic liner and absorbent material. Shippers should package their products with sufficient dry ice for at least twelve hours more than the expected transit time. Carriers discourage shipping perishable products over the weekend. Mark refrigerated containers with the following information: (1) name of refrigerant inside container, (2) amount of refrigerant inside container, and (3) product description. Table 6 provides a general rule of thumb for shipping frozen goods with dry ice.

Table 6: Average Amounts of Dry Ice Usage

Weight of Frozen Good	Time in Transit			
	4 Hours	12 Hours	24 Hours	2 Days
2 LB	2 LB Dry Ice	4 LB Dry Ice	8 LB Dry Ice	16 LB Dry Ice
5 LB	3 LB Dry Ice	6 LB Dry Ice	10 LB Dry Ice	18 LB Dry Ice
10 LB	4 LB Dry Ice	8 LB Dry Ice	14 LB Dry Ice	24 LB Dry Ice
20 LB	5 LB Dry Ice	10 LB Dry Ice	20 LB Dry Ice	30 LB Dry Ice
50 LB	10 LB Dry Ice	20 LB Dry Ice	35 LB Dry Ice	50 LB Dry Ice
NOTE: For each additional day add 8 to 15 pounds of Dry Ice.				

Source: Adapted from dryiceinfo.com web site, http://www.dryiceinfo.com/shipping.htm, accessed December 2009.

2.4.3 PROTECTIVE PACKAGING

The protective function of packaging essentially involves protecting container contents from the environment and the environment from the contents. The inward protective function is to ensure full retention of the utility value of the goods. A key objective of packaging is to protect the product from loss, damage, and theft. Packaging must be able to withstand different static and dynamic forces encountered during transport, handling, and storage. In addition, certain products require protection from humidity, solar radiation, temperature, and precipitation. The objectives of protective packaging will vary with products, customers, and mode of transportation. The following objectives commonly apply:[96]

1. Product Protection. The primary purpose of protective packaging is to insure the integrity and safety of the contents.
2. Ease of Handling and Storage. All areas of the distribution system should be able to process the packaged product economically.
3. Shipping Effectiveness. Container design should allow for the full utilization of the transport vehicle.
4. Ease of Identification. Container contents and special handling instructions should be readily identifiable.
5. Customer Needs. The container should provide ease of opening, dispensing, and meeting any special handling or storage requirements.
6. Environmental Awareness. Container design should allow for minimal waste and comply with governing regulations while satisfying customer requirements.

Perishables can be sensitive to temperature change and other factors that affect their shelf life. To retain their value in the marketplace, perishables must arrive at their destination in good condition. Like many other products, perishables require a certain degree of protection from hazardous elements associated with transport. It is critical to understand a product's temperature requirements and carefully monitor all procedures from packaging to storage to transportation. Properly designed, constructed, and utilized shipping containers will assist in protecting the product during transport. Shippers must be aware of adverse factors such as rough handling, improper stacking, moisture loss, and temperature fluctuations.

Rough handling. Containers with flawed design are more susceptible to collapse due to rough handling and high humidity conditions.

Improper Stacking. Overloading containers and stacking them beyond their design limit can cause damage to container and contents.

Moisture loss. Protect perishable products from exposure to high relative-humidity levels.

Temperature fluctuations. Adequately vented containers will promote proper airflow throughout the container.

Without packaging, most products would have a difficult and expensive journey through a shipper's supply chain. Shipping containers must provide physical qualities necessary to ensure the product survives normal bumps and jolts associated with transport. Protective packaging adds to the value of the product by lowering the transport cost. The goal of protective packaging is to provide an efficient and effective container design at minimal cost.

2.5 Hazardous Materials

The Department of Transportation (DOT) defines a hazardous material as "any article or substance having a clear potential for causing harm to any employee of the shipper, carrier, consignee, or regulatory agency exposed to the shipment."[97] Properly describing a hazardous material is a fundamental requirement for communicating the presence of a potential hazard to anyone exposed to the shipment. The description also provides specific emergency actions if an incident involving the material should occur. The description includes the DOT basic description and other information found in the Hazardous Materials Table, Title 49, Code of Federal Regulations. Information is necessary to complete documentation, labeling, certification, and container marking requirements. Information must appear on the "shipping paper" in the sequence shown in the chemical table or in an alternative sequence authorized by DOT Docket HM-215E.

2.5.1 HAZARDOUS MATERIAL REGULATIONS

The Hazardous Materials Transportation Act of 1975 (HMTA), as amended, is the major transportation-related statute regulating hazardous materials shipping. An objective of HMTA was to improve regulatory and enforcement authority of the secretary of transportation. HMTA empowers the secretary of transportation to designate as hazardous material any material that may pose an unreasonable risk to health and safety. Therefore, shippers should prepare and transport hazardous materials according to Federal Hazardous Materials Regulations (HMR). Hazardous material regulations are in Title 49 of the Code of Federal Regulations (49 CFR), Parts 100 to 185. The U.S. Department of Transportation enacts and enforces all hazardous materials transportation law in the United States. It has jurisdiction over interstate, intrastate, and foreign transportation of hazardous materials on aircraft, railcars, water vessels, and highway carriers and shippers in the United States. Following are four functional areas that cover hazardous materials regulations:[98]

- Procedures and Policies 49 CFR, Parts 101, 106, and 107
- Material Designations 49 CFR, Part 172

- Packaging Requirements 49 CFR, Parts 173, 178, 179, and 180
- Operations Rules 49 CFR, Parts 171, 173, 174, 175, 176, and 177

Regulations apply to any person who transports or causes transport or ships a hazardous material, or who manufacturers, fabricates, marks, maintains, reconditions, repairs, or tests a package or container represented, marked, certified, or sold by such persons for use in transporting hazardous materials. Enforcement of hazardous materials regulations is the responsibility of the following administrations under delegation from the secretary of the Department of Transportation (DOT):

Research and Special Programs Administration (RSPA). RSPA has authority over container manufacturers, reconditioners, and retesters, and shares authority over shippers of hazardous materials.

Federal Highway Administration (FHA). FHA enforces motor carrier regulations.

Federal Railroad Administration (FRA). FRA enforces rail carrier regulations.

Federal Aviation Administration (FAA). FAA enforces air carrier regulations.

Coast Guard. The Coast Guard enforces water-shipping regulations.

International Maritime Dangerous Goods code of regulations governs international shipments. Authorities of the countries who adopt the regulations enforce them. U.S. domestic and international regulations are similar in documentation, labeling, marking, and placarding requirements. However, some differences do exist. Whenever regulations conflict, the more stringent of the two will apply.

2.5.2 CLASSIFICATION

The mechanism for applying hazardous material regulations begins with classifying the hazardous material. This fundamental shipper responsibility consists of an analysis of scientific testing data to determine the characteristics of a material. To identify materials with dangerous properties, International Maritime Organization (IMO), a branch of the United Nations (UN), established nine dangerous goods classes. Some classes subdivide to provide further identification of a material's hazardous characteristic. Some materials have more than one hazard class. The order in which materials are numbered is for convenience and does not imply a relative degree of danger. Following are the nine hazard classes:[99]

- Class 1 – Explosives
- Class 2 – Compressed Gases
- Class 3 – Flammable Liquids
- Class 4 – Flammable Solids
- Class 5 – Oxidizing Substances and Organic Peroxide
- Class 6 – Toxic and Infectious Substances
- Class 7 – Radioactive Material
- Class 8 – Corrosives
- Class 9 – Miscellaneous Dangerous Goods

Chemical classifications are in the 49 CFR Hazardous Materials (HM) Table. It is shippers' responsibility to use established scientific criteria to classify their hazardous materials into one or more of nine classes.[100] Shippers must determine the appropriate description and packing group for their hazardous material from the chemical table. Basic descriptions in the chemical table identify chemicals regulated by DOT. For materials not classified, third-party testing facilities are available to perform these services.

2.5.3 MATERIAL DESIGNATION AND COMMUNICATION

The basic purpose of documenting a hazardous materials shipment is to provide the carrier with handling and emergency response information. The HM Table (49 CFR §172.101) designates which materials are hazardous. It also classifies each material and specifies the packaging, labeling, and transporting requirements. Hazardous material communications consist of documentation and identification of packaging and transport vehicles. Shippers communicate using markings, labeling and placarding, and shipping papers. Upon determining the proper shipping name, the Hazardous Material Table will specify correct packaging. The shipper is responsible for determining the proper shipping name (PSN).[101] Shipper must also specify the hazard class, United Nations Identification Number (if required), labels, packaging requirements, and quantity limitations.

Markings. Markings must establish clear communication about the material in a container. Persons offering for transport a hazardous material must ensure the container or transport vehicle shows the markings appropriate for the corresponding hazard. Specific rules and requirements are in 49 CFR §172.300. Basic marking requirements consist of proper shipping name and identification number of the hazardous material contained (see Figure 11). The shipper may not offer or transport a container unless HM markings apply to container contents.

Figure 11: UN Hazmat Marking

Source: Adapted from Federal Motor Carrier Safety Administration web site, http://www.fmcsa.dot.gov/safety-security/hazmat/complyhmregs.htm, accessed December 2009.

There is an exception for empty containers if (1) it is not visible and loaded and unloaded by a shipper or consignee, or (2) markings remain covered during transport. The following marking requirements apply:[102]

- Precede shipping name and identification with UN or NA number
- Technical name (if required)
- Shipper's name and address
- Consignee's name and address
- Orientation markings for liquids
- Place markings away from other markings and do not obstruct
- Apply legible markings in English
- Display markings on a background of sharply contrasting color

Class 9 materials are not in a hazard class, but may pose some degree of danger during transport. Class 9 materials (consumer commodities – paints, cosmetics, aerosols, medicines, nail polish) are referred to as ORM-D. They are marked as described in 49 CFR §172.316 according to the mode of transport selected. Other special marking requirements for shipments of certain radioactive and poisonous materials are in 49 CFR. Hazardous materials have assigned UN and NA numbers.[103] United Nations (UN) Numbers are four-digit numbers used worldwide in international commerce and transportation to identify hazardous chemicals or classes of hazardous materials. North American (NA) Numbers are identical to UN numbers.

Labeling and Placarding. Requirements for labeling hazardous material containers prepared for transport is in 49 CFR. This means each container must show the specific hazard label as displayed in the chemical table for the appropriate service. Labels and placards are a common approach to warning the public of hazards that may encounter. Figure 12 is an example of a DOT label, defined as 4" x 4" colored diamond with warning words and graphics. A placard is a 10.8" x 10.8" diamond-shaped sign placed on the four sides of a vehicle that carries hazardous material.[104] Labels communicate the same hazards for smaller containers offered for transport. Labels must meet specific requirements of §§172.411 through 172.448 in 49 CFR. These requirements specify the design, size, and color of the label. Exceptions to the hazard labeling requirements are in the "Ground and Air Packaging Provisions – Exceptions" column of the chemical table.

Specific label requirements are in the "Ground Shipments – Hazard Label Required" column. Some hazardous materials have multiple risks and require more than one hazard label. The first label name displayed is the "primary" risk class.[105] Additional label names are the "subrisks" for that material. Display subrisk labels on the same side of the container as the primary label and associated marking. If container size does not accommodate both primary and subrisk labels, affix subrisk label on an adjacent side within 6" of the primary label.

Figure 12: Oxidizing Materials Label

NOTE: The above label or placard designates a cargo that contains oxidizing materials (Division 5.1: Oxidizer and Division 5.2: Organic Peroxide). Placards are required when transporting over 1001 lbs. of oxidizers or organic peroxides.

Source: Adapted from Wikipedia web site, http://en.wikipedia.org/wiki/Dangerous_goods, accessed January 2010.

Shipping Papers. Shipping papers are used for day-to-day activities involved in the transport of hazardous materials. Whether the shipment is by ground or by air, "shipping papers" must accompany each hazardous material container. Shipping papers must contain information about the hazardous material as required by 49 CFR 172.201-203. DOT requires specific information, as shown below, on the shipping paper:

- Emergency telephone number (when required) §172.604
- Proper shipping name §172.202(a)(1)
- Class or division number §172.202(a)(2)
- Identification number §172.202(a)(3)
- Packing group number §172.202(a)(4)
- Quantity of material §172.202(a)(5)
- Other regulatory information such as "Limited Quantity" or "LTD Qty," DOT exemption number, and EX numbers
- Certification and signature §172.204(a)

Shipping papers must accurately describe and identify the hazardous material.[106] There are four items (see Figure 13) known as the hazardous materials basic description: proper shipping name, hazard class or division, identification (ID) number, and packing group.

Proper Shipping Name. Appropriate response to a hazardous incident depends on correct identification of the material. When transporting hazardous material, correctly spell the name of the hazardous material on the shipping papers.

Hazard Class or Division. The hazard class of a hazardous material is indicated by its class or division number, its class name, or by the letters "ORM-D."

ID Number. The four-digit identification number provides quick identification of all hazardous materials. Numbers preceded by "UN" are descriptions of materials for domestic and international shipments. Numbers preceded by "NA" describe material designated for shipments within the United States or between the U.S. and Canada.

Packing Group. This number is shown in Roman numerals. On shipping papers, the letters PG are entered before the number. Packing Group I indicates a high-level of danger while Packing Group III indicates the lowest danger.

If a hazardous material and a nonhazardous material show on the same shipping papers, the hazardous material must be: (1) named first (2) shown in contrasting color on all copies of the form, and (3) identified with an "X" in the column marked "HM." Entry must be legible and in English. When using more than one page, the first page must indicate multiple pages, for example, "page 1 of 3." Enter an emergency response telephone number on the shipping paper immediately after each hazardous material description. Shipping papers must contain the shipper's certification, which declares the container complies with HMR. Shipping papers serve as a manifest for hazardous materials picked up from a single address. The document authorizes carriers to transport hazardous materials to their facility.

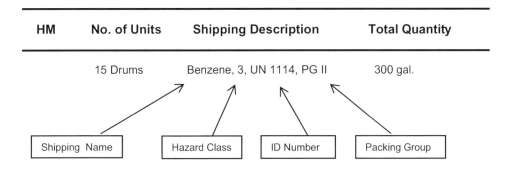

Figure 13: Example Shipping Paper - Benzene

Source: Based on National Oceanic and Atmospheric Administration (NOAA) Chemical Response Tool web site, http://chemtrsponsetool.noaa.gov/crt_home_page.htm, accessed December 2009.

2.5.4 PERFORMANCE ORIENTED PACKAGING (POP)

DOT 49 CFR §173.24 states that packaging for hazardous material must be sufficient to ensure material shipped is contained safely throughout the transport cycle. Shippers must be aware of "conditions incident to transportation" for their selected carrier and ensure proper packaging. Packaging hazardous materials for transport by aircraft is often more restrictive than for ground transport. Shippers must comply with packaging requirements for air shipments, as shown in 49 CFR §173.27. Provisions include performance requirements for Classes 4 and 8. Because of their unique system of moving containers, parcel carriers often require a higher level of packaging safety than DOT. Each hazardous material listed in the chemical table has an associated packaging authorization reference. *Reference* refers to the specific section of 49 CFR Part 173 that lists authorized components of performance packaging.

Performance oriented packaging (POP) was introduced into international packaging regulations in 1989 and became a requirement for U.S. shipments outside the continental United States (OCONUS) on January 1, 1991.[107] In 1996, POP became law of the land for packaging-regulated hazardous materials. POP consists of inner receptacles, cushioning, and absorbent materials, and an outer packaging designed and certified for containing specific hazardous material. It is important to test and implement packaging systems as designed. UN markings and identification numbers distinguish POP packaging components. See Appendix 5, Example UN Marking.

Packaging Requirements. Packing group of the material, its vapor pressure, and the chemical compatibility between the container and its hazardous material determine its packaging requirements. Performance tests determine non-bulk packaging standards. The United Nations (UN) recommended performance-oriented test, a vibration test for non-bulk packaging, is a domestic requirement. Container manufacturers submit written notification to customers of any specification shortfalls or steps required to conform to application specifications. Performance tests for UN packaging, including design qualification tests and periodic retest are in 49 CFR Part 178. The packing group designated in §172.101 (see Table 7) shows the degree of danger presented by the material.

Table 7: Packing Groups

Packing Group	Degree of Danger
I	Great
II	Medium
III	Minor

Source: Adapted from the Federal Motor Carrier Safety Administration (FMCSA) website, http://www.fmcsa.dot.gov/safety-security/hazmat/complyhmregs.htm#hm, accessed December 2009.

Shippers are responsible for classifying and describing hazardous material in accordance with 49 CFR Parts 172 and 173. This includes determining the appropriate packing group and applicable special requirements. It is the shipper's responsibility to insure its container adheres to hazardous material regulations regarding manufacturing, assembly, and marking. Shippers may accept manufacturer's certification, specification, approval, or exemption marking in determining packaging compliance. It is the responsibility of the packaging manufacturer and shipper of hazardous materials to assure containers can pass prescribed tests.

UN and DOT Package Certification. The process begins with an applicant submitting a container to an authorized Package Certification Agent (PCA) with a detailed description of packaging material specifications. Submission of engineering drawings of container assembly is a requirement. Without specifications, PCA will perform a detailed audit on all packaging materials. An applicant must submit all container assemblies needed by PCA for performance testing. Quantity submitted depends on the container type and certification requirements. For example, a 4G-combination container requires eleven complete containers. Prepare containers as they would be for normal shipping, except inner containers, which contain a non-hazardous substance, usually water. Some of the tests performed are as follows:[108]

1. Cobb Water Absorption Test. This is a corrugated box performance test.
2. Drop Test. This test requires a container drop from a specified height.
3. Stack Test. Loaded on the box is a weight equivalent to a three-meter stack of identical boxes.
4. Vibration Test. This is a test performed on a container to determine the acceleration that will cause it to fall off a test table.
5. Hydrostatic Pressure Test. This test is performed on an inner container that holds liquids and ships by air. The test involves bottles pressurized with water for a specified duration.
6. ISTA Test (Optional). This is a drop and vibration test required by some small parcel carriers.

Upon successful completion of required tests, PCA will issue a certification of compliance. This allows the applicant to apply UN markings to the complete container assembly. The applicant can expedite the certificate schedule by providing a detailed list of packaging materials and specifications with their container samples. After testing and certifying, containers will comply with UN and DOT standards for one to two years. Retesting the container is a requirement if it remains in use at the end of the certification period. It is the applicant's responsibility to make sure the container is in current certification status while in use.

2.5.5 STENCH PACKAGING

Some hazardous material can create an obnoxious and penetrating odor during transport that may contaminate other containers and pose an undue risk. It is typical for carriers to require a packaging system that protects against the release of odors in case of leakage from a primary receptacle. The following packaging components are the minimum required for containment of odors:[109]

- No more than one primary receptacle of glass, metal, or plastic
- Cushioning material
- Two intermediate containment systems of metal or plastic (for example, a metal can in a sealed plastic bag)
- Corrugated box of minimum 275 lb. Burst Strength or 44 ECT certification

Containers designed to ship a material requiring stench packaging must meet requirements set forth in 49 CFR for performance packaging. Stench packaging requirements do not apply if a packaging "exception" is in the chemical table for the material and material meets requirements of the exception. An "exception" is a permanent entry in the 49 CFR and does not have an expiration date. Exceptions allow some relaxation of regulatory requirements, but only under specific conditions.[110] Any company can use an exception without a written approval or application.

2.5.6 DOT EXEMPTION PACKAGING[111]

The Department of Transportation works on an *exemption* basis. Regulations forbid shipping hazardous materials without an exemption. An "exemption" is a written authorization from DOT, which permits a company or group of companies to do something not allowed in the regulation. An example is the use of non-specification packaging instead of the required specification packaging. A company must apply in writing for an exemption and submit a safety justification that is satisfactory to the DOT. An exemption has a life of up to two years. To extend or renew an exemption, a company must apply in writing for an extension. Application for an extension or renewal is due not less than sixty days before the expiration date specified in the exemption. If granted, exemption will specify if a copy must accompany each shipment. Unless stated otherwise, shippers must include the exemption number on each container used under its provisions. The "DOT-E" number must also appear on the shipping paper and shipper's certificate. An example of an exemption is LPS Industries DOT-SP-8249 exemption packaging system. This exemption allows LPS to legally ship hazardous materials without the "Toxic/Poison" label.[112] On November 25, 2005, the DOT changed its designation to DOT-SP-8249. SP stands for "Special Permit." The change did not affect the exempt status, only the DOT designation. This packaging system enables shippers to transport liquid and solid toxic poison materials in complete safety.

Exemptions issued by DOT are not acceptable in other countries (including Canada) unless issued as a Competent Authority Approval (CAA).[113] Shippers have to request a CAA and provide proof that will allow the Research and Special Programs Administration (RSPA) to determine if the request is safe and reasonable for international transportation. All countries, regardless of what country issues the CAA, accept CAAs.

2.6 Export Packaging

Export involves transporting goods to foreign markets by sea, air, or land transportation. When selecting a mode of shipping, it is important to consider product characteristics, such as size, value, destination, perishability, required speed of delivery, and transport cost. Compatibility with other elements of the distribution system, such as packaging, warehousing, inventory control, and handling should also influence the decision. Water (or ocean) shipping is the most common method of export shipping.[114] Bulk shipping is the transporting of commodities such as grain, logs, and fertilizer. Break-bulk water shipping is when products are loaded on and off by individual piece or a bundle of cargo, such as palletized load. With container shipping, the products are loaded into containers and moved from door-to-door without further handling. Air transport has become the mode of choice for shippers of high value products, exporters of perishable foods, and manufacturers replacing machinery or machinery parts. Generally, air shipments require less packing than ocean shipments and standard domestic packing is normally acceptable. Occasionally, carriers require the use of high-test (at least 250 pounds a square inch) cardboard or triwall construction boxes for air shipments.[115]

Shippers should be aware of four potential problems when designing their export shipping container: breakage, moisture, pilferage, and excess weight. Frequently, containers stack on top of or touch other containers. Often, overseas shipping facilities have conditions that make goods more susceptible to damage when moving through customs or in transit to the final destination. Moisture is always a concern because condensation can develop in the hold of a ship, even when equipped with air-conditioning and a dehumidifier. In addition, foreign ports do not always have enclosed storage facilities. Theft and pilferage are additional risks to guard against. Weight and volume are factors in determining transportation costs; therefore, consideration should be given to packaging that will minimize weight and volume.

2.6.1 PACKAGING STANDARDS

Export shipments typically require greater handling than domestic shipments. The International Organization for Standardization (ISO) and other consumer protection organizations have guidelines that assist exporters on how to minimize container weight and volume, avoid breakage, and theft proof their shipments. Many standard-setting organizations are associate members of the ISO, which means ISO standards represent their technical views as well.[116] Standards applicable to packaging are extensive and deal with matters as varied as performance tests, container type, size requirements, closure techniques, and compatibility.

Export shipping involves modes of transportation, packaging requirements, and documentation that differ from domestic shipping. A key objective of container design is product protection, from the assembly line to the user. Poor quality packaging can lead to damage and outright rejection of the shipment. The primary function of packaging is to protect the product from damage caused by contamination, crushing, breakage, weather, and theft, before, during, and after transport. Shippers should consider all factors that can adversely affect product safety during handling and storage at different stages of transport. Product factors to consider when deciding on packaging include fragility, durability, susceptibility to moisture, chemical reactions, shelf life, and mode of transport. Following are some common packaging standards:[117]

Dimensional Standards. These standards help to ensure the interchangeability of packaging components and accessories and assist in modular packaging design. Standards make it easier for consumers to compare container contents and cost.

Quality of Resistance to Wear Standards. These standards help ensure the product will meet its designed purpose.

Standard Test Methods. Standardized tests compare materials and products intended for the same purposes, for example, a test used to determine the breaking point of a corrugated box designed to transport a commodity by water.

Standardized Technical Terms and Symbols. These are terms and symbols adopted by industries as acceptable technical language readily understood within the industry.

Codes of Standard Practice. These codes recommend technical procedures for packaging methods used in a specific industry. While industrialized countries have adopted these codes, lesser-developed countries often use the codes as guidelines.

No universally accepted standards exist for pallets. Companies utilize hundreds of different pallet sizes around the globe. While no single dimensional standard governs pallet production, there are some widely used sizes. The International Organization for Standardization (ISO) sanctions six pallet dimensions, detailed in ISO Standard 6780: *Flat Pallets for Intercontinental Materials Handling – Principal Dimensions and Tolerances.* Of the top ten pallets used in North America, the most commonly used is the Grocery Manufacturers' Association (GMA) pallet.[118] GMA pallets accounts for 30 percent of all new wood pallets produced in the United States. The ISO also recognizes the GMA pallet footprint as one of its six standard sizes.

2.6.2 PACKAGING PROCESS

Before starting the packaging process, shippers should consider the possibility their shipment will be damaged. Frequent causes of damage are fragility, surface finish, rigidity, size and weight, and quantity packed. Shippers should establish their product's susceptibility to conditions such as water, water vapor, oxygen, heat, and cold. A thorough examination will help determine possible hazards to protect against during transport. Keep in mind the possibility that the product itself can cause damage. Shippers can enhance the likelihood their product will arrive at the destination intact by considering some basic issues.

Disassembly. The degree of product disassembly will affect a container's overall dimensions. Disassembly allows a reduction and simplification of protection against damage. While assembled, a product may require cushioning to protect the most fragile part. After disassembly, each part may only require cushioning to protect it.

Fragility. It is important to consider a product's inherent fragility. A question to answer, "Can the product withstand shock when cushioned within a container?"

Shipment Orientation. Often, products must ship *one way up* and are susceptible to damage or rendered useless when instructions are not followed.

Sensitivity to Field Forces. Certain products degrade when exposed to various forces, such as electrostatic, electromagnetic, and magnetic. These products include electronics, magnetic tape, high-speed film, and diskettes. Proper shielding and precautionary markings are necessary to protect these products.

Sensitivity to Temperature. There are products that are sensitive to extreme low and high temperature. For example, high temperature can affect chocolate candy while low temperature may affect computer diskettes.

Generally, the product's destination market determines packaging requirements. Shippers should understand these requirements and customize their packaging to conform. For example, most developed countries will not allow the import of fruit, vegetables, and meat in containers that do not eliminate the chance of contamination. Also, research the capabilities of the destination country to ensure there are adequate refrigeration, loading, and storage facilities. Keep in mind, materials used for shipping will vary according to the product, mode of transportation (truck, rail, ocean, or air), and ultimate destination.

2.6.3 MARKING AND LABELING

A good rule to follow is to mark and label containers clearly to prevent misunderstanding and delays in shipping. Stencil letters onto containers using waterproof ink. Markings should appear on three faces of the container, preferably on "top," the two "ends," or two "sides." Remove old markings and insure specific labeling and marking on export shipping cartons and containers (1) adhere to shipping regulations, (2) ensure proper handling, (3) conceal the identity of the contents, (4) help consignees identify shipments, and (5) insure compliance with safety and environmental regulations. Overseas buyers usually specify which export markings should appear on the cargo. Following are examples of markings required on export shipments:[119]

- Shipper's mark
- Country of origin
- Weight marking (shown in pounds and kilograms)

- Number of containers and size (shown in inches and centimeters)
- Handling marks (international pictorial symbols)
- Cautionary markings, such as "This Side Up" (in English and language of destination country
- Port of entry
- Labels for hazardous materials (universal symbols adapted by the International Air Transport Association and International Maritime Organization)
- Ingredients, if applicable (in the language of the destination country)

Markings and special handling instructions should include the total number of containers in the shipment, when applicable. It is wise to repeat all instructions in the language of the destination country and use standard international shipping and handling symbols. Customs officials strictly enforce regulations governing freight labeling. As an example, many countries require the country of origin labeled on each imported container. Because of the complexities involved in the export process, export shippers rely on international freight forwarders and export packing specialist to perform many of the required services.

2.6.4 UNITIZATION

"Unit" concept or "unitization" is a basic principle of packaging.[120] Unitization allows handling of goods by mechanical equipment throughout the distribution network. In practice, unit concept means to enclose small, expensive items in wood boxes, or double-, even triple-wall containers to avoid pilferage and damage. Secure large items directly to a pallet and use shrink-wrap or steel strapping to secure smaller boxes and other containers to a pallet. Before selecting packaging material, consider factors such as temperature, humidity, packaging strength, buyer requirements, graphics, labeling, freight rates, and government regulations. Following are basic exporting procedures:[121]

1. Properly cushion or block items within the container to prevent moving or rubbing against other products.
2. Select the most advantageous pallet size and style. Four-way entry pallets permit handling from all four sides with a forklift or pallet truck. The standard pallet size, 40" x 48" maximizes the volume that can be loaded into a shipping container.
3. Prepare ferrous surfaces with a rust inhibitor to prevent rust or corrosion.
4. Insert holes in the skid or floor area of large containers, boxes, or crates to allow seawater or condensation to drain.
5. Use waterproof ink and keep markings to a minimum. Refrain from adding trademarks or product descriptions to the box. Apply "cautionary markings" in English, language of the destination country, and appropriate international graphic-handling symbol.

2.6.5 PALLETS

A pallet is a flat transport structure designed to support goods in a stable fashion while being lifted by a mobile device, such as a forklift.[122] Pallets (or skids) made of wood and plastic meet specific handling and loading requirements. The advantages of plastic pallets are chemical and moisture resistant, clean easily, are lighter, and do not splinter. While plastic pallets are more durable, wood pallets are cheaper and more common. Pallet size is the overall pallet dimensions expressed as pallet length x pallet width (see Figure 14).

Figure 14: Basic Pallet Design

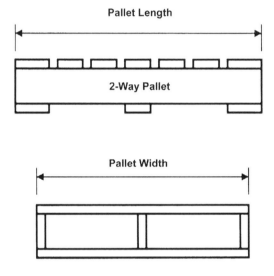

Source: Based on National Wood Pallet & Construction Association article, "Pallet Classification" http://www.nwpca.com/pds/palletclassification.pdf, accessed August 2010.

2.7 Shipping Containers

A key objective when transporting parcels (or small packages) is to provide protection while expediting safe and cost-effective product distribution. Small parcels carriers encounter a wide range of shipping hazards that differ from larger truckload and rail shipping. Both automatic and manual handling can result in dropped parcels. Shock is potentially damaging to products. Lateral impact against container walls, down chutes, or while moving along conveyors is also hazardous to small parcel shipping. Small parcel shipping does not require unitized or pallet load setup. Without added protection, realized from the safety of numbers, parcels grouped on pallets often encounter higher stress levels.

Typically, small parcel carriers' conveyor sort systems handle corrugated boxes since they are the dominant shipping container. Carriers use auxiliary systems, such as carts, pallets, and slower moving conveyors, to sort other types of containers such as bags, tubes, and wood boxes. Many products ship safely and economically in containers other than corrugated boxes. Each container has its own set of advantages and limitations. A prudent guideline is to use a container appropriate to the product's shipping requirements. Many companies have packaging groups or rely on "third-party" professional packagers to provide a container design that will meet their shipping needs.

2.8 Corrugated Boxes

It is estimated that corrugated boxes comprise more than 90 percent of all shipping containers moving by truck, rail, and air. Corrugated boxes, commonly used for custom-manufactured shipping containers, packaging and displays, is durable and lightweight. Corrugated cardboard is made of paper and has a ruffy layer (called *fluting*) between smooth sheets called *liners* (see Figure 15). The corrugated cardboard most commonly used to make boxes has one layer of fluting between two smooth sheets. There are many types of corrugated material available, each with different flute sizes and thickness. Corrugated material is the preferred packaging material because it is high-tech, customizable, protective, graphically appealing, cost-effective, and environmentally friendly.[123]

High-Tech. To reduce cost and insure consistent performance, manufacturers use computer-aided equipment to design and manufacture corrugated components and products.

Customizable. Manufacturers customize corrugated material into an unlimited array of shapes and sizes for specific product protection. Users of corrugated material can have high-resolution color graphics (including lithography and silk-screening) printed to meet specific purposes.

Protective. Corrugated material offers excellent tear, tensile, and burst strength that allow it to withstand shipping pressures. It resists impact, drop, and vibration damage while offering uniform stacking and weight distribution.

Graphically Appealing. Corrugated boxes and packaging are mobile billboards that create product image. Corrugated material is a flexible medium that accommodates a wide range of printing options:

- Offset lithography and rotogravure (high-volume)
- Flexography or letterpress (shorter runs)
- Silk-screening (displays)
- Direct printed in plant
- Manufacturing with a high-end color graphics process

Cost-Effective. Corrugated boxes are one of the least expensive shipping containers. The cost of labor and tools required to produce, fill, and move a corrugated box is low in comparison to other types of containers. There is a significant cost reduction when using corrugated material as an all-in-one shipping, storage, advertising, and display medium.

Environmentally Friendly. Corrugated material is a natural, renewable material and has a good environmental record. Corrugated boxes use a high percentage of secondary fiber (including old boxes, old newspapers, and straw) for manufacture. Corrugated material has the highest recycling rate of any packaging material.

Figure 15: Corrugated Fluting

Single-wall   Double-wall

Source: Based on The Center for Unit Load Design at Virginia Tech article, "What Pallet Manufacturers Should Know About Corrugated Boxes!", http://www.unitload.vt.edu/technote/980918/980918.htm. accessed August 2010.

2.8.1 TYPES OF CORRUGATED BOXES[124]

Corrugated material converts into styles and shapes from simple "slotted" styles and intricate point-of-purchase displays, to multipart containers involving interior packaging. Regular Slotted Containers (RSCs) are the most common box style and are economical to manufacture (see Figure 16). An RSC has four flaps on the bottom and an identical arrangement on the top. The RSC box blank has all flaps cut the same depth. All flaps are the same length and meet at the center of the box. When sealed, only the two outer flaps are visible.

Variable Depth Boxes. Variable depth boxes are similar to RSCs boxes but the height of the variable is adjustable.

Figure 16: Regular Slotted Container (RSC)

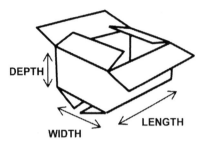

NOTE: Generally, RSC's shipped to the user flat. When needed, the user squares up the box, inserts the product and seals the flaps

---

Mailers. Mailers are flat boxes with hinged lids. A flat mailer is stronger than an RSC box of the same shape. Some mailers have dust flaps on the lid to keep out dust. Other style mailers have locking tabs that allow the front flap to close on the outside. Figure 17 illustrates some common mailers.

Figure 17: Flat Mailers

 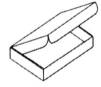

Economy Style Tuck Top   Roll End Dust Flaps with Locking Tabs   Roll End Tuck Top Dust Flaps

---

Folders. Adjustable folders work like a box and an envelope. Like a variable depth box, the height is adjustable. Folders provide more protection than an envelope but less than an RSC box. Five-panel folders are long, thin, square corrugated boxes commonly used in place of round mailing tubes. While not as strong as mailing tubes, they will not roll off conveyor belts. Three-sided folders fold to form a triangular cross-section instead of the more conventional square type. A three-sided figure will not fold over and collapse as easily as a four-sided figure. The larger flat side permits use of larger, more legible labels. Figure 18 illustrates some common folders.

Figure 18: Folders

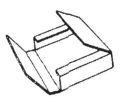 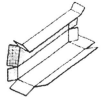 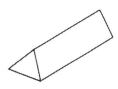

Adjustable Folder   5-Panel Folder   3-Sided Folder

2.8.2 BOX DIMENSIONS

Box dimensions follow the sequence of length, width, and depth (or height), either for inside or outside the box. Box length is the longest of the side panels at the opening (see Figure 19). Box width is the shorter dimension. Box depth is perpendicular to the length and width. Generally, box size indicates inside dimensions (ID). Accurate inside dimensions ensures a proper fit for the product shipped or stored. To approximate outside dimensions (OD) add three-eighths of an inch to the single wall inside box dimensions, three-quarter inch for double wall boxes, and one and an eighth inch for triple wall boxes. The most economical box size for a given cubic volume has Length:Width:Depth proportions of 2:1:2.[125] For example, an RSC that measures 10" x 5" x 10" is the most efficient size to obtain 500 cubic inches of box volume. For example, an RSC that measures 25 x 5 x 4 inches, which is also 500 cubic inches, will use 20 percent more corrugated board. There are instances when less efficient box dimensions will satisfy product requirements or marketing strategies.

Figure 19: Box Dimentions

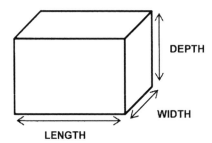

NOTE: Box dimensions are given in the following order – length, width, and depth.

2.8.3 BOX PERFORMANCE

Historically, carriers have regulated the transport of corrugated boxes—Rule 41 for rail and Item 222 for truck.[126] These rules apply to the minimum grades of fiberboard required to carry specified maximum weights and sizes. Early 1991, carriers amended their rules by offering an alternative to the old "test" grades if shippers wished to use an alternative grade.[127] The alternative was "ECT" fiberboard, a material measured for its edgewise compressive strength by the Edge Crust Test. ECT offers a different determination than the old Mullen (burst) test. The burst test examines rough handling durability of fiberboard while ECT correlates to the stacking strength. There are two gages of strength used for corrugated boxes: box compression strength and stacking strength. Box compression strength (BCT) is the maximum load a box can stand for a moment. Stacking strength is the maximum load a box can stand throughout the distribution cycle. The bottom box must support a top load exposed to fluctuations in temperature and humidity. See Table 8, Box Strength Guidelines

Table 8: Box Strength Guidelines

Maximum Weight of Contents (lbs.)	Size Limit of Box (inches) (L + W + D)	Bursting Test (lbs. per sq. in.)	Edge Crush Test (ECT) (lbs. per in. width)
Single Wall Corrugated Containers			
30	75	200	32
40	75	200	40

50	85	250	44
65	95	275	55
80	105	350	NA
Double Wall Corrugated Containers			
60	85	200	48
80	95	275	51
100	105	350	61
120	110	400	71
140	115	500	82
150	120	600	NA

Source: Adapted from IoPP Transport Packaging Committee, Guide to Packaging for Small Parcel Shipments, (03/01/02), http://www.iopp.org/files/SmallParcelPackagingRev1204.pdf.

Other factors, such as handling, pallet patterns, pallet deck board spacing, and overhang, may affect a box's performance. The *McKee* formula provides a compression strength estimate of a given box. By knowing the compression strength, a box designer can determine the ECT test required to achieve the desired stacking strength. A corrugated box may carry the old Mullen burst strength rating or the ECT rating. ECT boxes of the same grade level will have a higher stacking strength than burst boxes, but less tensile and tear strength for rough handling durability. If stacking problems exist, using the ECT specification is a viable alternative. Burst or puncture test specification is an alternative if the issue is containment strength and puncture resistance.

2.8.4 BOX MANUFACTURER'S CERTIFICATE (BMC)

Box Manufacturer's Certificates (BMCs) are markings that indicate the box meets material requirements stated in the BMC and structural requirements of Item 222 and Rule 41.[128] Trucking companies and railroads require BMCs as an indication of certified minimum strength for a maximum allowable gross weight and overall box dimensions. There are two types of BMCs (see Figure 20).

Figure 20: Type of BMC's

```
              PACKAGE CERTIFICATE
    THIS BOX MEETS ALL CONSTRUCTION REQUIREMENTS
         OF APPLICABLE FREIGHT CLASSIFICATION

    FOR PACKAGE NO     BURSTING TEST LBS PER SQ IN
```

Source: Based on National Motor Freight Classification (NMFC), STB NMF 100-2 (November 1999), Item 222-1, —Specification for Fiberboard Boxes Certification of Box Manufacturer‖ and Item 299, —Numbered Packages-Authorization and Certification.

Circular types are for boxes that meet the general requirements of Item 222 or Rule 41. Rectangular types are for those that meet the specifications for a Numbered Package. Burst (Mullen) and ECT grades of fiberboard are acceptable for corrugated fiberboard box use in small parcel systems. However, the two grades have different properties that may reflect in their performance during transport. The purpose of burst grade fiberboard is to provide tensile and tear strength. ECT grade fiberboard provides a high-level of crush resistance. While sufficient stacking strength is an important attribute required in small parcel systems, durability is just as important. A corrugated fiberboard box must retain and protect its contents during manual and automated handling. The National Motor Freight Classification and Uniform Freight Classification use BMCs as enforcement tools to assess damage claim insurance. Exceeding the gross weight limit almost guarantees the carrier will refuse a claim if a shipment is damage. See Figure 21, BMC Basic Rules.

Figure 21: BMC Basic Rules

BMCs Must State:	Other BMC Rules:
• Name and location of the certification entity • Minimum material specification certified (edge crush test, or burst strength and basis weight) • Gross weight and size limits if it is an Item 222 or Rule 41 box • Package number if it is a Numbered Package	• BMC must be on the outside surface. • Circular BMCs must be three inches in diameter (plus or minus one-fourth of an inch). A reduced size is allowed for small boxes as specified in either Item 222 or Rule 41. • Rectangular BMCs must be three and one-half by two inches (plus or minus one-fourth of an inch).

Source: National Motor Freight Traffic Association National Motor Freight Classification (NMFC), Item 222 and the National Railroad Freight Committee's Uniform Freight Classification (UFC), Rule 41.

2.9 Other Shipping Containers

A key consideration in selecting proper packaging material is the compatibility between the material and product packaged. Because of the infinite combination of product formulas and container materials, buyers are responsible for testing their containers to assure compatibility. Compatibility refers to how a product affects the container (stress, cracking, paneling, swelling, corrosion, rust buildup). Permeability involves the loss of product through the container sidewalls and leakage of moisture into the container.

2.9.1 DRUMS AND CANS

Drums are classified as interior or exterior containers and reusable and non-reusable containers; they are cylindrical, straight-walled containers manufactured out of material such as steel, plastic, and fiber.[129] Drums can have rolling hoops pressed or expanded from the body of the drum or L-bars welded to the body. Drums may have removable or non-removable heads. Drums can be "open head" or "tight head." An open head drum has a removable lid secured on the drum with a locking band. Some open head containers have a lug cover crimped on. A tight head drum, used for water and other liquid products, does not have a removable lid. Open head drums are primarily for dry products. Drums come in various sizes: 5, 30, 55, 85, and 110 gallon. Certification is required for drums used to transport hazardous material. A certified drum must adhere to the UN rating specific to the hazardous material it contains.[130] **Cans** are used for vacuum or pressurized packaging. Cans come in various shapes and sizes and are made of metal, paperboard, pulp board, or a combination of materials.

2.9.2 BARRELS

There are three basic types of barrels: plastic, steel, and cardboard. *Plastic* barrels are useful in that they are reusable for water or other types of storage. A plastic barrel beveled at the top and bottom has a decreasing capacity. *Steel* barrels are the strongest barrel, which means they can carry the most weight, but can rust if dented. *Cardboard* barrels are of little use after shipping, but are inexpensive and common. Before choosing a cardboard barrel, it is best to decide its intended use. Ship heavy items in a barrel that is heavy (has thicker sides) and a steel bottom. Use barrels with cardboard bottoms to ship light items. Barrels come in an array of sizes, categorized as follows:[131]

- Jumbo barrels measure taller than 38 inches.
- Regular barrels are between 27 and 38 inches tall.
- Small barrels are shorter than 27 inches.

CAUTION – When buying a *used* barrel, check for damage caused by denting, cutting, or water. Water damage leaves a discoloration. Also, beware of "cable" barrels used to ship cable wiring. They have a cone in the center that holds cable in place. Removal of the cone can weaken the bottom.

2.9.3 STEEL PAILS

Millions of steel pails produced in the U.S. each year range from one to twelve gallons (3.8-45.4 L). There are four basic configurations: (1) full open-head, straight side, lug cover, (2) full open-head, nesting, lug cover, (3) tight-head, straight side, and (4) tight-head dome top. Liquids, viscous products, powders, and solids are some items stored and transported in pails. The market for pails include paint, printing inks, chemicals, adhesives, cement, roofing materials, petroleum products, janitorial supplies, and a score of other products. Pails can withstand extreme temperatures, which make them the container of choice for transporting and storing flammable and combustible liquids.

2.9.4 SACKS[132]

Over eight thousand people work to produce paper sacks in the United States, a billion dollar a year industry. More than two thousand different products use sacks as packaging. Paper sacks are flexible containers made from three to six or more walls of specification paper and other material. Custom-designed sacks meet specific requirements and provide a high degree of product protection at a low cost. Manufacturing plants print product graphics on the outer ply of a sack with clarity and detail. Sacks come in many sizes, as specified by the shipper, and are consistent with suppliers' manufacturing capability. Multiwall sack capabilities range from twenty pounds to 110 pounds of product. There are two basic types of sacks constructed for use according to the filling method:

- Open Mouth – Filling is by gravity or compression.
- Valve – Filling is through a tube or spout.

Generally, sack plants fabricate *valve* sacks except for a corner opening to allow filling at the customer's packing plant. These same plants fabricate *open mouth* sacks, except for the top. Greater use of sacks with a greater value-per-pound will occur as improvements in materials, construction, and distribution systems continue to develop.

2.9.5 BAGS

For direct-to-customer shipments of non-breakable items, shipping bags are an option. It is common for retailers to use bags and other flexible packaging to ship items, such as clothing, linens, and other soft goods, to their customers. It is common to ship office supplies, paper products, books, electronic media, and mail-order pharmaceuticals in bags. In comparison to corrugated boxes, bags cost less, weigh less, and require less storage space. Bags are not appropriate for shipping items that need a high level of protection. Shipping bags can be plain, reinforced, padded, bubble, foam, plastic, or corrugated reinforced, and come in various sizes and styles. Shippers should consider the following when purchasing shipping bags:[133]

- Correct style and size
- Lip or tape closure
- Whether it is strong enough to handle product weight

The goal is to use a bag that will allow the item to ship damage free. Inappropriate use of bags can result in damaged goods and increased costs.

2.9.6 TUBES[134]

Shippers use tubes to ship artwork, maps, blueprints, posters, and large documents they do not want folded. They come in various sizes, shapes, and materials. Typically, companies that stock tubes carry tubes with diameters of 1-1/2 inch, 2 inch, 2-1/2 inch, 3 inch and 4 inch. Standard lengths range from 6 to 48 inches. Paper tubes made of fiberboard, composite materials, paperboard, and Kraft paper are lightweight, rigid, and come in three main styles: open-end, snap seal, and telescopic. Tubes do not have to be cylindrical; they can be square, rectangular, triangular, or cone-shaped.

Open-End. These are made of heavy three-ply, spiral-wound paperboard with a tight fitting plastic cap that seals the end of the shipping tube to provide strength.

Snap Seal. These tubes do not use any external end caps. Instead, the ends fold in to seal the tube. They are economical and do not require tape to keep them closed.

Telescopic. These tubes adjust to hold different size documents. They have metal end caps and are almost crush proof.

Paper tubes offer numerous benefits, some of which are (1) protection from condensation, (2) sturdiness and flexibility, (3) recyclable material, (4) little expense, and (5) tolerance to extreme temperatures.

2.10 ESD-Protective Packaging

Many of us have experienced occurrences of electrostatic discharge. Electrostatic discharge (ESD) is the sudden and momentary electric current that flows between two objects at different electrical potentials.[135] Often, people are the prime generators of static electricity. The simple act of walking around or repairing an ESDS device can generate several thousand volts on the human body. If not properly controlled, static electricity can discharge and damage a sensitive electronic device. This is called a human body model (HBM) discharge.[136] While personnel-generated static is typically the primary ESD cause in many environments, automated manufacturing and test equipment also pose a problem. For example, when a device slides down a feeder, a rapid discharge can occur if it touches a metal object. This is called a charged device model (CDM). Improper packaging of ESD sensitive (ESDS) components, assemblies, and equipment, resulting in hard and soft failures, has cost manufacturers and users millions of dollars. Considering the expense of assemblies, it makes economic sense to incorporate effective ESD protective packaging. The following is a list of common static electricity sources:[137]

- Work surfaces – waxed, painted or plastic
- Floors – waxed, vinyl tile, sealed concrete
- Clothes – smocks, nonconductive shoes, synthetic materials
- Chairs – vinyl, fiberglass, finished wood
- Packaging – plastic bags, foam, trays, tote bags
- Assembly area – spray cleaners, heat guns, blowers, plastic tools

Packaging materials, such as bags, corrugated, rigid, and semi-rigid packages, provide direct protection of ESDS devices from electrostatic discharge. The primary use of these items is to protect the device when it leaves the facility, usually when shipped to a customer. Materials-handling products such as tote boxes and other containers provide protection during inter- or intra-facility transport. For a container to be effective, it must offer certain electrical, chemical, and mechanical characteristics. Static shield plastic bags have become a popular way to package assemblies and components.[138] The main function of ESD packaging is to limit the possible impact of ESD from turboelectric (static caused by the contact and separation of similar or dissimilar material) charge generation, direct discharge, and electrostatic fields. ESD containers allow shippers to store and transport sensitive electronic components safely outside an Electrostatic Protective Area (EPA). A key element in a static control program is the use of appropriate symbols to identify static-sensitive devices and assemblies. ESD Association standard "ANSI ESD S8.1-1993–ESD Awareness Symbols" provides two symbols for ESD identification.[139]

2.11 Pre-Shipment Container Testing

Pre-shipment tests can be a useful tool when used properly. The most effective time to utilize a pre-shipment test is prior to shipping or packaging design changes. This will allow for potential problems to be identified and solved before shipment. Test results are only as good as the test procedure performed. Some results of performing the wrong tests include inaccurate test findings, over packaging (thus, over spending), and shipment damage. Common pre-shipment tests are box drop, box vibration, compression on box, and atmospheric preconditioning. The tests recommended for small parcels are free-fall drop, incline impact, random vibration, repetitive shock vibration, machine compression, and constant load compression. Container manufacturers should evaluate each container's ability to protect the product throughout handling, distribution, and the storage environment. A container must be able to distribute the product without damage and retain it in the correct orientation for proper removal and use.

The American Society for Testing and Materials (ASTM) and the International Safe Transit Association (ISTA) are principal sources for methods of container testing. ASTM has one performance test protocol (D4169) devoted to packaged-product performance in distribution.[140] It is a pre-shipment general simulation test covering a range of package types and distribution scenarios. Typically, testing to ASTM D4169 involves rather sophisticated, extensive, and expensive equipment, and skilled operators. ISTA offers a variety of test protocols, often tailored to specific situations. Mainstream ISTA tests are pre-shipment test procedures to compare or evaluate effectiveness of protective packaging and a packaged product's ability to withstand the hazards of distribution. ISTA classifies procedures and projects in Series.[141] Different Series give users a choice of cost, complexity, and operator skill requirement.

2.11.1 ASTM D4169

Damage often occurs because shippers do not provide adequate packaging to protect against excessive force imposed on containers during transport. ASTM has developed a method to determine what is "adequate" or "excessive" in its standard D4169. This standard gives packaging designers a way to predict how a new or redesigned container will perform. It provides a uniform basis of evaluation by subjecting shipping containers to a test plan of predictable hazard elements. This performance approach is a systematic way to (1) define desired attributes of a packaged item, and (2) determine if it adequately fulfills those requirements without regard to the specific materials used. Within specified performance standards, producers should manufacture a container that is both cost-effective and safe.

Testing. Testing subjects a container unit to a sequence of hazardous elements such as shock, drop, vibration, and compression. Test plans provide a uniform basis of evaluating the ability of a shipping unit and its contents to withstand the distribution environment. It is important to understand the expected product distribution before designing a customized distribution cycle (DC). For example, the DC used in the small parcel overnight shipping environment for medical device containers is DC13. A unique feature of D4169 is its flexibility in determining the intensity of a test. There are three levels available for all test methods based on the assurance level required to achieve package performance:[142]

- Level I – highest assurance
- Level II – average or medium assurance
- Level III – lowest assurance

The assurance level selected depends on factors such as tolerable damage, number of units shipped, and knowledge of product environment. Level II is used for most goods while shippers of high-value items or critical-care products may desire a higher assurance for their packaged products and select Level I. Packaging cost incurred depends on the desired level of assurance. Generally, Level I requirements will incur a higher cost for packaging, but higher assurance of acceptable performance is often worth the added cost.

2.11.2 ISTA PRE-SHIPMENT TEST PROCEDURE

The International Safe Transit Association (ISTA) is an international leader in advancing the science of packaging and the use of performance testing. ISTA Pre-shipment Test Procedures provide a means for manufacturers to predetermine the probability of the safe arrival of their packaged products at the destination. Tests simulate shock and stress commonly encountered during shipping. Pre-shipment tests are a useful tool when applied properly. The most effective time to utilize these tests is before shipment of the product or before changing container or product design. ISTA will certify tests results when performed in an ISTA certified laboratory using ISTA procedures. Due to their unique system of moving packages, parcel carriers often require a higher level of packaging safety than the Department of Transportation (DOT) and International Air Transport Association (IATA). For example, in addition to DOT or IATA requirements, packages submitted to UPS must meet ISTA Procedure 1A test protocol requirements.[143] ISTA provides an additional test standard (ISTA Procedure 3A – accepted by UPS but not required) specific to small package transportation.

ISTA 1 Series Non-Simulation Integrity Performance Tests challenge the strength and robustness of product and package combination and are useful as screening tests, but do not simulate environment occurrences.

Procedure 1A: Packaged-products weighing 150 lb (68 kg) or less. Basics requirements are fixed displacement vibration and shock testing.

ISTA 3 Series General Simulation Performance Tests provide a laboratory simulation of damage-producing motions, forces, conditions, and sequences of transport environments. Characteristics include simple shaped random vibrations and different drop heights applied to sample packages, as well as atmospheric conditioning such as tropical wet or winter frozen.

<u>Procedure 3A:</u> Packaged-products for Parcel Delivery System shipments 70kg (150 lb) or less (standard, small, flat, or elongated). Basic requirements are atmospheric conditioning, random vibration with and without top load, and shock testing. Effective 2006, Procedure 3A superseded Procedures 3C and 3D; 3A encompassed and updated both Procedures.

ISTA confines its technical activities to packaged products. Products and containers are tested together as a unit. Ideally, tests should include multiple shipments to each of several destinations. Containers are inspected on arrival at the destination or returned unopened to the point of origin for inspection. If there is an analysis of the damage, lab test results may be necessary to determine the cause. Depending on the damage incurred, findings may indicate a need to intensify lab tests.

2.11.3 ISTA 3A 2004 TEST

When designing packaging for a particular product, packaging engineers and carriers attempt to develop a container that will pass ISTA (International Safe Transit Association) 3A, 2004 test. The purpose of the test is to evaluate a container's ability to protect a product when shipped in a parcel distribution environment such as FedEx and UPS. While this test procedure includes a series of different tests, an important piece of information to keep in mind is the expected heights a product may drop. If the container can withstand a drop from heights indicated in Table 9, it is reasonably certain the product will ship damage free.

Table 9: Drop Height Test

Product Weight	Average Expected Drop Height	Worse Case Drop Height
Less than 70 pounds	18 inches	36 inches
70 –150 pounds	12 inches	24 inches
Over 150 pounds	N/A	N/A

Source: Adapted from PackagingPrice.com article, "How do I package my product for shipping?," http://www.packagingprice.com, accessed April 2008.

2.12 Vendor Packaging Compliance

Vendor compliance is at the heart of efficient supply chain management. Shippers often lack control over their suppliers when it comes to packaging. To assist shippers in holding their vendors accountable for providing adequate packaging, major parcel carriers have developed *vendor packaging compliance* programs. These programs assist manufacturers, and suppliers facilitate change at the point of origin. Container performance testing is efficient in controlling damage, by encouraging the use of effective packing materials and packing methods. There are numerous benefits to implementing a vendor compliance program:[144]

- Ensures packaging meets acceptable performance standards
- Eliminates need for costly over-packing and double-boxing
- Streamlines picking, packing, and shipping processes
- Lowers operating costs

Establishing and monitoring vendor compliance is a team effort. Rationalizing vendor relations poses a significant challenge. Vendor compliance works best when a company can clearly state to its vendors consistent parameters and goals—and just as important, specific sanctions for noncompliance. Vendor compliance guidelines should clearly outline details of packaging requirements. Guidelines should outline the process and timeline for vendors to undertake necessary corrections to meet established requirements. Creating a vendor compliance manual will require an investment in time but will help eliminate confusion. If the expertise to write a packaging compliance manual does not exist in-house, seek third-party assistance. Implementing a vendor compliance program and enforcing it can be rewarding.

SECTION III – MANAGING PARCEL SHIPMENTS

3.0 Basic Considerations

3.1 Parcel Pricing Components

3.2 Multicarrier Shipping Solutions

3.3 Selecting a Carrier

3.4 Freight Audit and Payment

3.5 Accessorial Charges

3.6 Size and Weight Restrictions

3.7 Shipment Consolidation

3.8 Loss, Damage, and Delay Claims

3.9 Contracting

SECTION III

MANAGING PARCEL SHIPMENTS

TODAY'S COMPETITIVE BUSINESS ENVIRONMENT brings many issues and challenges to parcel shippers. Companies, especially small- to mid-size companies, must continuously improve their shipping process to remain competitive, or risk losing customers and profits. When evaluating the existing shipping environment, one key area for organizational improvement is the shipping department. In the electronic age, it is now possible for shippers to know a lot about their parcel shipping process. Shippers can take an active role in managing their parcel shipping to increase efficiencies and take extra costs out of their shipping budget. Timely and damage-free delivery can mean the difference between satisfied customers, customer complaints, and goods that customers return. Companies should understand their customers' needs and communicate to them clear delivery expectations. Shipping can have a dramatic impact on the cost of doing business, and by following proven guidelines, managers are better able to control costs and improve customer loyalty. In today's competitive business environment, managing shipping costs is essential to the future success of a business.

3.0 Basic Considerations

Regardless of the type and quantity of parcels shipped or the selected carrier, the following are some basic considerations:

- Delivery schedules
- Service guarantees and refunds
- Delivery date
- Routing guidelines for returns

Delivery schedules. Monday through Friday are normal delivery days. If a parcel ships on Friday, the scheduled delivery day is Monday, not Saturday. A Saturday delivery will cost extra. The U.S. Postal Service is the exception. USPS considers Saturday a normal delivery day for Standard and Priority parcels. USPS will delivery Express mail seven days a week to an address that is not remote. An important feature of carriers' websites is the ground service maps.

Service guarantees and refunds. Delivery commitment can be valuable information when choosing a carrier. Knowing how each carrier will service a specific delivery will help in the decision-making process. Monitoring the delivery of a shipment is not always an efficient use of labor time. Therefore, outsourcing this process to a company that monitors shipments electronically can provide valuable information about a carrier's performance. Information gathered will help identify customer delivery problems.

Delivery date. A carrier's EDI billing statement should list the delivery date and time. This information is available on carrier websites, which provide easy links to shipment tracking and customer service numbers.

Routing guidelines for returns. Easy-to-follow instructions on how to return an order conveys a customer-friendly environment and is essential to customer satisfaction. On the other hand, vendors are knowledgeable when it comes to shipping and have little problem following more detailed routing instructions.

3.1 Parcel Pricing Components

It is important for shippers to understand their shipping characteristics and parcel carriers' pricing strategies. Certain characteristics are more attractive to carriers than others, mainly because they yield higher profits. Carriers desire business that includes high-margin, premium shipments, as well as shipments that are cheap to handle. An example would be large volumes of parcels delivered to a single destination that is close to a major distribution hub. Carriers are more likely to show flexibility with discounts on high-margin business than they are on low-margin shipments such as rural and home deliveries. Following are key components used to price shipments:[145]

3.1.1 PUBLISHED AND NEGOTIATED RATES

Published (or no discount) rates apply to shippers who have no established pricing agreement with a carrier. This would typically be someone who walks into a FedEx office or UPS store to ship a parcel. On the other hand, a **negotiated** rate is a rate the shipper has negotiated with a carrier ahead of time. Factors in the marketplace have an effect on negotiated rates. Generally, negotiated rates contain service level discounts, volume incentives, and net or gross spend rebates. Factors that improve a shipper's ability to negotiated favorable rates are package volume and characteristics, zone density, net or gross spend, and the ability to negotiate.

3.1.2 DELIVERY OPTIONS

A key component to consider when identifying shipping costs is carriers' *delivery options*, also called *service offerings*. It is important to consider distinct delivery options and price variation between residential and business (commercial) locations. For example, a "2nd-day" delivery could mean a 4:30 PM delivery time to a business location and a 7 PM delivery time to a residential location.[146] The shipping rate for a parcel shipped to a residence will be higher than a parcel shipped to a business location. While expedited delivery options such as *overnight* and *same-day guarantees* are profitable for carriers, for shippers, a short time frame may not be necessary. The cost variation between the next day at 10:30 AM and the next day at 3 PM can be considerable. Cost-conscious shippers will use expedited services sparingly while relying on lower cost delivery options. This will provide a time-definite delivery guarantee at a fraction of the cost. Shippers should determine which delivery options are cost-effective in meeting their established goals and objectives.

3.1.3 WEIGHT AND ZONE PRICING

Until the mid-1990s, it was common practice for carriers to base their shipping charge for a given parcel on weight. Under this pricing strategy, a parcel, regardless of content, would cost the same shipped across country or across the street. In 1996, UPS introduced zone-based pricing for its overnight parcel delivery service.[147] FedEx, the company that pioneered overnight delivery, launched its zone-based rate in 1997. This meant that depending on the destination, a parcel shipped within the continental United States would incur one of eight different charges. While zone-based pricing decreased the cost of shipping to nearby locations, it increased the cost of shipping long-distance. Parcel carriers who use a zone and weight-based pricing formula divide weight into one-pound increments, typically from one to 150 pounds. The United States and the world are divided into a series of shipping zones. Origin address zone and destination address zone determine the shipping charge.

Table 10, Domestic Ground Commercial Rates, illustrates a parcel carrier's zone system. The rate table shows one-pound increments, up to 150 pounds. The farther a zone's distance from another zone, the longer transit time and higher shipping cost. A shipper's address determines the origin zone. A Baltimore, Maryland, zone table is different from a Newark, New Jersey, zone table. As shown in Table 10, a ten-pound package shipped to Zone 5 would be $6.96 and a thirty-pound shipment to Zone 2 would be $8.78. Charges shown in the zone table are for transportation only and do not include accessorial charges. Zone numbers used by one carrier do not necessarily apply to another carrier.

Table 10: Domestic Ground Commercial Rates

Weight	Zone 2	Zone 3	Zone 4	Zone 5	Zone 6	Zone 7	Zone 8
1	4.20	4.32	4.46	4.65	4.89	4.97	5.08
10	5.59	5.71	6.44	6.96	7.56	8.51	9.61
20	6.96	7.87	8.22	9.51	11.97	14.39	16.85
30	8.78	10.20	11.20	13.18	17.06	20.11	24.36
40	10.34	12.55	14.16	16.90	21.83	25.81	30.90
...	...	...	...	...	...	...	...
150	62.90	65.29	67.23	67.81	72.44	78.74	83.54

NOTE: Carriers use different zone designations. For example, Zone 44 for UPS may not be the same zone designation for FedEx or DHL

3.1.4 PARCEL CHARACTERISTICS

The characteristics of a parcel, such as shape, size, and weight, play a key role in determining shipping cost. Historically, gross weight (pounds or kilograms) determined the shipping cost. As the cost of crude oil increased, carriers began to realize that charging solely by weight was becoming increasingly unprofitable. The space occupied by low-density shipments was not in proportion to its weight. *Dimensional* weight is a uniform means of establishing a minimum charge for the cubic space a shipment occupies.[148] Dimensional weight calculates the volumetric weight of a parcel. Carriers use the greater of actual weight or dimensional weight to calculate a shipping charge. Dimensional weight is the parcel's dimensions (length x width x height) divided by factor 194.[149] International shipments use factor 166 to determine weight.

Shippers can manage the impact of dimensional weight charges by reducing packing material and the size of their parcel, when possible.[150] Eliminating the need for a box is another packaging strategy. Often, padded and non-padded mailers are adequate for shipping products safely. It may also be possible to shrink-wrap the product instead of shipping it in a corrugated box. As shipping costs continue to increase, it is important for shippers to analyze their parcel characteristics and consider solutions that focus on greater cube efficiencies.

3.1.5 ACCESSORIAL CHARGES

A key factor to consider in transportation pricing is *accessorial* charges, often referred to as surcharges, ancillary charges, adjustments, and value-added service fees. There are over eighty accessorial charges, and to manage shipping costs, it is important to understand them.[151] Some accessorial charges incremental to the transport of commodities are residential delivery, address correction, oversize charges, reconsignment or rerouting, weekend pickup or delivery, and detention, just to name a few. Carefully manage accessorial charges, which represent a significant portion of a shipper's transportation spend. Shippers should identify their specific service requirements and include accessorial charges as part of the transportation contract discussions.

3.1.6 FUEL SURCHARGE

During the mid-1990s truckload carriers added a surcharge to freight charges to address the rapid rise in fuel prices, rather than increase their freight rates. Carriers reasoned that by adding a variable surcharge instead of raising freight rates, they would gain a competitive advantage during periods when fuel prices declined. Carriers also considered this approach fairer to their regular customers. Before long, other segments of the transport industry, including parcel carriers, began adding a fuel surcharge to their freight charges. Fuel surcharges have become a major component of the transport charge, with carriers free to determine their own fuel surcharge rate. Typically, carriers base their fuel charge on the current U.S. National Average Diesel Fuel Index price of diesel fuel, combined with their own method for computing freight charges.[152] Parcel carriers categorize fuel surcharge as ground and express. Generally, diesel fuel price determines the ground surcharge and jet fuel price determines the express surcharge.

Fuel surcharge impacts the cost of goods sold, and like freight charges, can vary from carrier to carrier. Carriers' fuel surcharges have risen sharply, as have the price of oil. Fuel surcharge has a cost recovery and profit generation component that is negotiable. Awareness of what other companies' fuel surcharges are can enhance a shipper's negotiating position. Shippers can negotiate to have a fuel surcharge rate cap if fuel cost reaches a certain level. While carriers' fuel surcharges are likely to remain, by negotiating with carriers, shippers can strategically manage their fuel surcharge spend.

3.1.7 SERVICE CHARGES

Service charges are a small component of pricing and do not affect the cost of an individual shipment as accessorial or surcharges do. Typical service charges are *weekly pickup* and *late payment.* Shippers can access their carrier's website to become familiar with their charges and take precautions to reduce the impact on their transportation costs.

3.2 Multicarrier Shipping Solutions[153]

Selecting the right carrier can be a challenge. Carriers have different niches that they serve and offer options and charges specifically related to those selections. No single carrier is the most cost-effective in all categories. For example, the U.S. Postal Service offers the best rates on lightweight residential shipments while Emery is competitive with heavyweight air shipments. DHL may have the most competitive international shipping rates. Even within the same mode of shipping, carriers often have different charges for the same shipping options. Awareness of carriers' shipping terminology and services offered is necessary to ensure the best service at the most reasonable cost. Often, in a small company, the shipping manager will wear more than one hat and does not always have the time or expertise to shop every parcel shipment. What can further complicate shipping is a process called "Non-production Shipping."

With "Production Shipping," shipping is routine and predictable. Production shipping involves professionals and their support staff who deal with shipping issues, negotiate contract rates, and manage costs. "Non-production Shipping" involves plans, proposals, contracts, and other types of documents sent to customers, suppliers, distributors, and vendors, often against an urgent deadline. Non-production shipping is unpredictable, difficult to control, and can have an enormous impact on costs. Workers not familiar with shipping may create errors or order services without knowing the cost or alternatives. An example of an error that can cause an additional service charge would be mislabeling or incomplete labeling.

3.2.1 INTERNET-BASED SOLUTIONS

One way to improve performance and reduce shipping cost is to utilize existing technology. By implementing a certified multicarrier shipping solution, shippers can access the provider's technology assets. For example, iShip Inc., a multicarrier shipping service, allows customers to price, ship, track, and manage their shipments over the Internet by use of a browser.[154] A multicarrier shipping service provides tools that assist shippers increase productivity, save money, and manage their shipping activities more efficiently. Multicarrier shipping services are typically provided through alliances with major carriers in the parcel delivery industry. Multicarrier service capabilities generally provide a set of built-in backup options if a particular carrier experiences a service disruption.

3.2.2 SOLUTION FEATURES

Multicarrier software solutions give shippers an ability to compare service options and lower transportation costs without compromising delivery requirements. Shipping solutions are a key component to cost-effective shipping and provide businesses with value-added shipping service. Real-time decision-making reduces costly errors, enhances productivity, and controls shipping costs. Solutions are stand-alone applications or are integrated into an organization's existing systems, such as Enterprise Resource Planning (ERP), Management Reporting System (MRP), Transportation Management System (TMS), and Warehouse Management System (WMS), to facilitate information transfer between systems. Following are some benefits provided by multicarrier shipping solutions.[155]

Carrier Selection. Shippers can access a rate and service matrix to select a carrier based on cost, delivery requirements, and customer preference.

Carrier Rate Comparison. Using individual carrier applications can make the task of comparing shipping rates difficult and time-consuming. Multicarrier solutions compare carrier rates and allows users to rate shop and analyze delivery alternatives.

Address Cleansing Correction. Some solutions integrate an address-cleansing feature that assists in providing a deliverable address. This feature reduces costs associated with carriers' address correction services and returns.

Integrated Tracking and Reporting. This feature provides real-time shipping status updates such as location and expected arrival time. E-mail and fax shipment notification features provide parcel-shipping status.

Generate Management Reports. Data gathered from shipping locations provides input for management reports.

Weight Management. This feature allows a shipper to compare expected versus actual weight.

Management Policy. This feature gives management the ability to specify shipping rules and procedures for all of its locations, and the ability to monitor compliance with company policy.

Efficient transportation delivery systems are critical to customer satisfaction and a company's success. Consolidation of shipping history creates the information base necessary to enter productive carrier negotiations. Shipping solutions make the job of shipping more efficient, reduces costs, and brings shipping under management control. Multicarrier shipping solutions are tools designed to assist managers leverage information and technology. Value-added resellers (VARS) assist shippers in reviewing offerings and matching their business requirements to the appropriate solution.[156] Trained VARS representatives work with customers on the implementation, integration, and training needed to obtain the maximum performance from their multicarrier shipping solution.

3.3 Selecting a Carrier

As shippers seek to develop core carrier relationships, the process of selecting carriers has become an important but time-consuming task. Factors that influence carrier selection are customer requirements, carrier dissatisfaction, and changes in distribution patterns. Information gathered helps determine which available option best meets the shipper's service requirements, at an acceptable cost. Attributes such as on-time pickup and delivery, damage-free delivery, accurate invoicing, consistent transit times, prompt response to inquiries, and competitive rates are important when evaluating and selecting a carrier. During the selection process, shippers often employ techniques such as cost studies, audits, and review of carriers' on-time pickup and delivery performance. Often, shippers will statistically analyze the quality of carrier service attributes, such as loss-damage ratios.

Understanding differences in carriers' terminology and services is necessary to ensure the best service. Analyzing and processing carrier differences are important when making informed shipping decisions. Individuals responsible for making carrier selection decisions do not always have an understanding and knowledge of carriers' service offerings. In small- to medium-sized companies, shipping managers commonly wears more than one hat and do not have sufficient time to shop every parcel shipment. Software solutions designed to assist shipping managers define the parameters of their shipments and what delivery requirements are available.[157]

3.3.1 PARCEL DELIVERY ALTERNATIVES

When selecting a carrier, there are *regional parcel carriers* to keep in mind.[158] There are five major regional carriers in the U.S.[159] For example, Eastern Connection, while small in comparison to UPS or FedEx, provides parcel delivery service in cities from Maine to Virginia. Less-than-truckload (LTL) carriers have become serious competitors in the domestic parcel delivery industry. Major LTL carriers offer services, such as time-specific delivery and tracking, historically associated with parcel carriers. Companies that ship most of their parcels to residences have the choice of using *consolidation and mail services*. Shippers can realize savings by having their parcels moved most of the way by truck and then given to the U.S. Postal Service for final delivery. This service is a variation of zone skipping, where consolidators place parcels into either UPS's or USPS's network at the end of line-haul and near delivery point. Parcel Direct (now known as FedEx SmartPost) is a parcel consolidator that provides services to companies that mainly ship residential. PFI (acquired by Parcel Direct) operates on the West Coast and specializes in daily delivery of parcels direct to USPS's "destination delivery units." Another group of providers includes *drop-shippers* and *logistics providers*. Drop Shippers primarily deal with flats and parcels. Using private carriers or express mail, they drop parcels into USPS's local Sectional Center Facilities (SCFs), Destination Delivery Units (DDUs), and Bulk Mail Centers (BMCs). Three major players are, Drop

Ship Express, RMX, and SmartMail. Logistics providers (LPs) work with carriers and large shippers to offer region-to-region services at the lowest cost.

3.3.2 CRITICAL ELEMENTS

Many small businesses, including e-businesses, use integrated carriers such as FedEx and UPS, which offer and set their rates for seamless door-to-door delivery service.[160] Using integrated carriers is the simplest method of getting goods to customers as they take care of routing, transfers, air transport, and duties. Even with this rather trouble-free shipping, there are key elements to consider when dealing with carriers—insurance, claims, shipping rates, routing, transit time, customer requirements, and tracking. It is important to understand how a carrier will address these elements before making a selection.

Insurance. Integrated carriers commonly insure a parcel for $100 (U.S.), which may or may not cover potential losses. Shippers can purchase "excess value" insurance against loss, damage, and delay in transit.[161] For example, FedEx offers "Declared Value Exception" service, which allows customers to declare a value up to $50,000 on special items such as jewelry, gemstones, and precious metals. Shippers should not assume that domestic insurance coverage would automatically cover a shipment once it crosses U.S. borders. Clarify origin point and destination point of the carrier's insurance coverage to insure it covers the shipment from door-to-door.

Claims. It is important for consignees to note all damages while the driver is still on site. The driver should also note damages on the delivery receipt. A consignee should inform the shipper of damage or loss and retain all packing material. Pursuing a damage claim is the shipper's responsibility. It is up to the shipper to file a claim in writing for payment of a specified or determinable amount of money. Documentation to support a claim includes pick up record, original invoice, documents that prove property value, and the extent of loss or damage. Carriers often find that a claim is the result of improper packing and refuse claim. A carrier's report will state the reason for denying claim. If a shipper disagrees with the report, it can request a second inspection. Collecting on a claim is one area where persistence can make the difference.

Shipping Rates. Weight (actual or volumetric) is the primary rate determinant. A carrier's truck capacity limits shipment volume as well as weight. Carriers use a "cubic rule" to insure they are charging for the space occupied and apply the greater of actual or volumetric weight. Carriers apply additional charges to cover extra charges involved in handling shipments. Following are factors that may be cause for additional charges:

- Articles not fully enclosed in an outer container
- Articles enclosed in a wooden or metallic shipping container
- Cans or pails not enclosed in another shipping container
- Parcel exceeds carrier maximum length limit

When shipping internationally, keep in mind that the destination country's import fees often come in many forms: province, port (water and air), and train station to name a few. Ask the carrier if there will be any surprise fees and if it has factored unforeseen charges into the rates.

Routing. Door-to-door service appears seamless when, in fact, the shipment may travel by a combination of ship, train, plane, and truck. To reduce costs, carriers move parcels to a hub, consolidate with other freight, and dispatch to the appropriate destination. Usually, the carrier selected will make routing decisions based on requested service. Shippers should know their carriers' routing channels, and if there is concern, they should discuss alternative routing with the carriers.

Transit Time. Transit time is the time that elapses between the departure of a shipment from its origin to its arrival at destination. This period is an estimate of each leg of the movement and any delays that may occur in between. Carriers can provide a zone sheet that delineates the time it takes a parcel to move from one zone to another. Ground service, which uses trucks and trains to move a parcel, may provide a cost-effective solution if shipper and client are in the same zone and time is not critical. Expedited service is an option if time is critical. Carrier service guides are a valuable source of information when it comes to comparing carrier transit times. The following are examples of common service categories:

- Early Next Morning – delivery before 9 AM next business day
- Next Morning – delivery before 10:30 AM next business day
- Next Day – delivery before 4 PM next business day
- Two Day – delivery before 4 PM second business day
- Three Day – delivery before 4 PM third business day

Domestic delivery transit time estimates are dependable when carrier traffic patterns run frequently. However, international shipments are another story. It is important to question a carrier regarding its overseas delivery time estimates. Carriers should be able to provide a list of international transit times to countries serviced, as well as a list of countries not served.

Customer Requirements. When a customer requests a "must arrive by" date and time, the shipper should allocate time for the initial processing (pick and pack) and when the carrier will show up. For example, an order that is compiled and transferred to an order-fulfillment warehouse on a Tuesday morning may not ship until Wednesday. Keep in mind, a carrier may count day one of transit time as the day after picking up the merchandise. It is important to select the right service. For example, why spend extra money for "next morning" service when "next day" would suffice. Shippers should discuss with their carrier pickup and delivery times prior to shipping.

Tracking. Carriers and shippers use tracking numbers to identify and track a shipment as it moves through the carrier's system. There are available shipping solutions that track parcels across multiple carriers. Shippers should include an itemized packing slip with their shipment and provide customers an order number, which will enable them to track their goods.

3.4 Freight Audit and Payment[162]

Increasingly, companies have come to realize the importance of an effective audit and freight payment process. Auditing is more than just refunds for late deliveries. Reports generated from the auditing process are equally important. Properly prepared reports provide managers valuable information. Reports are a valuable tool for controlling and managing *cost reduction* (address corrections and recurring surcharges) and *cost recovery* (billing errors and service guarantees). Audits identify errors and enable shippers to cut costs and improve their transportation function. The audit process serves an important role in controlling transportation costs and drives additional value-added services. Managers should thoroughly understand the audit process and communicate its importance to all appropriate parties. Audits function as a control utility and have many meanings, some of which are:

- Examination of bills for accuracy
- Correction of shipping charge
- Shipping contract and freight bill comparison

Delayed or missed freight bill payments occur when shippers consider audit and billing as a noncore business function. Carriers may factor in consistently late payments when negotiating future contracts. Timely and accurate freight bill audit and payment is necessary for cost avoidance and cost reduction.

3.4.1 TYPES OF AUDIT AND PAYMENT FIRMS

The freight payment industry developed in the mid-1950s as banks began to include freight payment as part of their cash management services. Growth was slow, but the early 1980s was the major turning point when freight audit firms became a small industry. Deregulation of the freight transportation industry and explosion of management information technology added complexity to the freight payment function. As a result, many companies found that keeping freight audit and payment in-house was unrealistic and turned to freight audit and payment firms. Following are types of audit and payment firms.

Freight Pre-Audit. Audit firms operate as traditional service bureaus. They audit carrier freight bills and forwarded them to the customer for further handling.

Post Audit. Firms audit freight bills after they have been paid and, if necessary, file overcharge claims on behalf of their clients.

Pre-Audit and Payment. Firms audit bills to determine freight charge and submit payment to the carrier. The shipper issues payment to the audit and payment firm.

Audit, Payment, and Information Reporting. Firms process freight bills in the same manner as the other firms previously mentioned. In addition, these firms generate reports from freight bill data.

After deciding to outsource audit and payment activities, the company will need to decide on a third-party payer (3PP) or a third-party logistics (3PL) provider. This decision rests on the company's overall strategy. Larger firms may feel there is greater value in working with third-party logistics firms because of their logistics expertise and ability to share logistics resources. Others may feel a freight audit and payment firm would be more effective at performing audits and payment activities.

3.4.2 ISSUES AND CONCERNS

Numerous incidents of payment problems associated with slow and nonpayment of freight bills by freight audit and payment firms have occurred.[163] Identify payment issues early and investigate allegations concerning slow or nonpayment of freight charges. Another issue is excessive cost because of a constant stream of rejected freight bills by the audit firm. This problem arises when the audit firm is unable to determine validity of the bill, its rates, and charges or general ledger codes. Often, this problem results in an audit firm billing the same freight bill many times to compensate for previous audit deficiencies. To perform a proper and complete freight bill audit, a detailed examination of shipping records must take place. This activity compares a shipper's bill of lading to the carrier's documentation, such as freight bill, delivery receipt, and weight certificate. The objective of the examination is to confirm the freight bill (invoice) represents the correct origin, destination, weight, ship date, commodity shipped, and who (shipper or consignee) is liable for freight charges.

It is important that shippers take advantage of their freight audit and payment process as an optimization tool. Timely audit of freight invoices can yield valuable information and serve as an important benchmark during carrier contract negotiations. Detailed account coding, made possible by an effective freight audit and payment system, helps to ensure proper allocation of freight costs. Freight invoice processing is time consuming, expensive, and often confusing. Often, a firm will not have staff or expertise to perform activities required for timely freight bill payment. When dealing with concerns and needs, a shipper should use an effective selection process for choosing its audit and payment firm.

3.4.3 OUTSOURCING

Many small- to mid-size companies cannot handle their freight audit and payment function in an efficient and cost-effective manner. Developing and managing carrier relationships require an intimate knowledge of the industry as well as knowledge of carrier tariffs and rates. To acquire this knowledge is time-consuming and often lost through employee attrition. Information required to process freight bills for payment constantly changes and requires much time to maintain a current knowledge base. Many companies find that issuing one check a week or month to a third-party instead of one check to each carrier is a cost and time-saver. For *third-party providers*, capital investment related to freight audit and payment is critical to their existence, which is reason to invest in the technologies, methodologies, and people necessary to audit and pay freight bills. Freight audit and payment providers provide rate and traffic data necessary for decision-making and evaluating carrier selection and performance.[164]

Outsourcing should begin with identifying needs.[165] When outsourcing a function, it is critical to follow a *best practice* approach to identify, select, and manage a third-party relationship. A clear understanding of desired objectives is necessary to determine if the provider can provide required services. Following are some basic issues to considered,

- What functions need outsourcing?
- What are the company's expectations?
- Who are the relevant third-party providers?
- What agreement should the company sign?

Before outsourcing, it is important for management to focus on its company's *characteristics, objectives*, and *performance.*

Characteristics. This is the awareness of present and future forecasts related to product flow, product handling, and packaging requirements, origin and destinations points, delivery cycle times, customer requirements, procedures for returns, hours of operation, and other related factors.

Objectives. Clearly outline objectives and specify who will be responsible for managing the program.

Performance. Define a baseline of costs and performance to evaluate "before" and "after" costs and performance.

It is important for management to be aware of the effect outsourcing can have on the company and involve all departments when establishing requirements and objectives. Information gathering and informal meetings with third-party providers will help identify which providers show promise to be a good match for the company. It is essential that management share information about the company's current situation and expectations with the prospective provider.

3.4.4 SELECTING A PROVIDER

Selecting the wrong vendor can be more costly to a company than processing its own freight bills. Once a company decides to outsource its audit and payment function, it will need to decide whether to work with a third-party payer or a third-party logistics provider. The decision will hinge on the company's overall strategy. Consider the following criteria when selecting a service provider: *financial strength, customer needs, technology,* and *information access.*[166]

Financial Strength. A first-rate freight audit and payment provider should have robust data management and delivery capability. In addition, it should have the financial strength to handle a large volume of freight bills. It is important to know the depth and experience of the provider's management staff and the stability and quality of its workforce. Following are some considerations when evaluating a potential provider.

- How long has company been in business?
- How many transactions does it handle annually?
- How many customers does it have?
- How many carriers does it work with?
- Is an audited financial statement available?
- Does the company provide risk protection?
- Is the company public or privately owned?
- Does the company provide fiduciary responsibility?

An experienced and reputable provider will demonstrate financial strength and have a record of accomplishments that indicate it can live up to its commitment. Data gathered will assist in determining the experience a provider will bring to the table.

Customer Needs. Management should consider a capable third-party provider who demonstrates a willingness to understand its company's entire supply chain. This will reflect on the provider's ability to look at the company as a unique entity and develop guidelines to meet its specific needs.

Technology. A provider should possess a thorough understanding of related technologies, as well as knowledge of its own industry's technology. A provider should incorporate current technological features and values within its field of expertise. A provider should commit to investing in technology to maintain a high "efficiency of scale." Questions should be asked to determine if a provider has the ability to adapt technologies to meet clients' needs.

Information Access. Third-party providers should be able to provide data relevant to the freight audit and payment process. Data reports must be of value and easily accessed. Questions should be asked to determine a provider's ability to convey client-specific information that will help the company better manage its freight audit and payment activities.

3.4.5 AUTOMATING THE PROCESS

Before management solution software, companies relied heavily on traditional systems that required manual audit and bill payment. The traditional approach was replete with an extensive history of issues and concerns. Often, transportation expenses, such as rating, scheduling, documenting, tracking, and auditing, were unknown and difficult to budget. Innovative managers realized that to have an effective logistics function, they would require an effective solution that gave them the ability to account for costs. Shippers looked to Internet applications from carriers, forwarders, third-party logistics companies (3PLs), and other intermediaries to perform services.

The Aggregator Solution. Aggregator refers to the manner in which web-based companies offer shippers a choice of carriers and access to carrier rates.[167] Much of the aggregator market is centered on individual consumers and small business owners and heavily reliant on parcel carriers to provide delivery service. For example, SmartShip.com, a California company targets both the business-to-consumer (B2C) and business-to-business (B2B) markets for parcel shipping.[168] Carriers' web-based tools provide shippers the ability to print labels and shipping documents, find rates, locate drop-off sites, and track shipments. Using an application-programming interface (APIs), aggregators are able to streamline buying and shipping tasks. Aggregators offer their services through web-based merchants, e-retailers, and auction sites. From the shippers' view, aggregation websites provide a convenient single-site service. From the service providers' view, aggregation can lead to greater productivity for asset-based carriers.

The ASP Model. An Application Service Provider (ASP) provides its services over the Internet and, generally, the operating software and data files reside on the provider's equipment. ASP audit, payment, and information service providers offer shipment information and cost control portals on their websites. Once the customer loads the tariffs and rates, the ASP system will automatically audit and process the freight bills. Shipping information is available 24/7 compared with traditional models, which require users to wait for their information. ASP systems provide service verification, prerating, and duplicate bill payment prevention. Users control their freight payment by simply letting the system know when to pay. An ideal ASP model is capable of the following:[169]

1. Accepting data, generating bills of lading, and retaining data for future use
2. Assigning transportation accounting codes
3. Creating files necessary to expedite shipping activities, such as tracking, auditing, duplicate payment prevention, freight payment, and performance monitoring

ASP's shipping functionality gives shippers the ability to compare carriers' services and rates. Shippers provide the recipient's information, which includes delivery date and shipment weight. The ASP system provides a display of the best shipping options from which to choose, and then completes the shipping transaction by printing all required documents.

After the package is on the way, the system's *tracking* function provides an e-mail notification of any potential problem or delay. Shippers can check a shipment status by simply searching on data elements such as consignee name, company, and address. A system's *service monitoring* function checks billing accuracy, service compliance, and delivery exceptions while accelerating invoice processing and payment to carriers. A system's *reporting* and *data warehousing* functions provide an analysis of the user's shipping activities, which can be used to optimize shipping activities.

3.5 Accessorial Charges

Parcel carriers have accumulated years of data and are imposing accessorial charges as they get a better fix on their operating costs. Carriers are aware of shipments that are cheap to delivery, such as a truckload of parcels delivered to a single city block near the carrier's hub. Carriers also know that shippers who routinely ship to remote locations or request numerous extras are more expensive to service. Armed with specific cost-to-serve information, carriers do not hesitate to recoup costs, in the form of service charges or accessorial fees. Collecting accessorial charges allow carriers to recoup the added costs they incur for hard-to-deliver shipments. In addition, fees and accessorial charges allow carriers to raise revenue without announcing a rate increase. Accessorial charges fall under three basic categories.

1. Accessorial charges designed to instill shipping discipline are address corrections, special handling for parcels exceeding size and weight limits, missing account numbers, and weight corrections.
2. Additional charges for value-added service include charges such as proof of delivery, collect on deliver (C.O.D.), sort and segregate, inside pickup and delivery, and notification.
3. Accessorial charges for shipments that result in additional carrier operating costs include hazardous material, oversize parcels, and delivery to residential and rural areas.

3.5.1 PURPOSE

Accessorial charges allow carriers to increase operating revenue without raising rates across the board. These charges make rates fairer because only users of the extra services pay the additional cost. In other cases, the fees apply to all shipments as a way of passing along the extra cost associated with doing business. *Fuel Surcharge* is a good example of an accessorial charge applied to most shipments. Parcel carriers reserve the right to impose a fuel surcharge and change the rate monthly. Some carriers use a monthly-adjusted index-based fuel surcharge.[170] Other carriers use fuel prices published by the U.S. Department of Energy to calculate their monthly fuel surcharge for ground and express services.

3.5.2 MONITOR AND CONTROL

Monitor, control, and quickly address accessorial charges if they fall outside an acceptable tolerance. Questioning the validity of an accessorial charge is often appropriate. For example, shippers frequently send more than one parcel to the same customer. While one parcel will have a complete address, the other parcel may be missing something irrelevant such as a suite number. The carrier may apply an incorrect address charge for the parcel missing the suite number. Dispute these charges when they occur. To reduce the financial effect of accessorial charges, many shippers have looked at opportunities to file claims for billing errors, such as guaranteed service failures and disputed residential surcharges. Understanding carriers' additional service fees can help shippers eliminate or lower costs.[171] Changes to minimize accessorial charges can be internal or external. For example, an address database will determine if an address is residential or business. Shippers should implement procedures to insure shipping weights are correct. Reduce insurance charges by obtaining insurance through reliable third-party insurance companies. Accessorial charges are negotiable, but a carrier may not be willing to negotiate if the shipper cannot provide historical shipping data.

3.6 Size and Weight Restrictions

Parcel size and weight is a key factor in determining the shipping rate. Carriers publish Terms and Conditions (T&Cs) that list their size and weight limits. It is the shipper's responsibility to determine if its shipments meet established limits. Carriers rate large, heavy, and odd-shaped parcels higher if they exceed their size limits. Restrictions apply to individual parcels but there is no limit placed on the total weight of a shipment or the number of parcels in a shipment. Table 11 summarizes weight and dimension restrictions for UPS, FedEx, and the U.S. Postal Service.

Table 11: Weight and Size Limits

Carrier	Maximum Weight (pounds)	Maximum Length (inches)	Maximum Length & Girth (inches)
UPS	150	108	165
FedEx	150	119	165
USPS (Parcel Post)	70	----	130
USPS (Priority Mail)	70	----	108

Source: Based on IsHIP, Inc., "Learn More – Weights, Dimensions, and Packaging," http://www.iship.com/priceit/info.asp?info=4, accessed April 2008.

The weight of a parcel includes weight of the item, container, and packing material. An accurate shipping charge is dependent on an accurate measurement and weight. To determine if a parcel is *oversize*, it is necessary to take two measurements: (1) length – the longest side of a parcel or object and (2) girth – two times the width plus two times the height or the measurement around the largest area of a cylinder. See Figure 22, How to Measure Length and Girth.

Figure 22: How to Measure Length and Girth

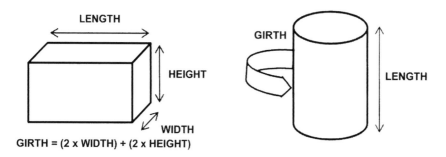

Source: Adapted from DHL-USA, "Determining Weight, Dimensions, Cubic Inches and Girth", http://www.dhl-usa.com/IntlSvcs/dimweight/dimweight.asp?nav=Inttools/DimWeiCal, accessed February 2010.

3.6.1 OVERSIZE PARCELS

Although most standard parcel shipping carriers will transport larger, heavier items, they usually charge a higher rate for them.[172] Typically, parcel carriers offer three types of oversized packages, called Oversized 1, Oversized 2, and Oversized 3. The problem of shipping large objects is a thing of the past. Today, there is a wide array of choices to choose from when it comes to shipping large objects. Table 12 outlines oversized parcel conditions.

Table 12: Oversized Ground Delivery Parcels

	Oversize 1 (OS1)	Oversize 2 (OS2)	Oversize 3 (OS3)
Parcel's combined length and girth exceeds (inches)	84	108	130
Parcel's combined length and girth is equal to or less than (inches)	108	130	165
Parcel's actual weight is less than (pounds)	30	70	90
Billable weight in (pounds)	30	70	90

Source: Based on Logisticsmgmt.com, "Pay attention to packaging!," http://www.logisticsmgmt.com/index.asp?layout=articlePrint&articleID=CA6343727, accessed April 2008.

3.6.2 DIMENSIONAL WEIGHT

Dimensional weight is a standard formula used in the airfreight industry to consider density when determining charges.[173] The International Air Transportation Association (IATA) sets the volumetric standard for dimensional weight. Volumetric calculations determine the space occupied versus the actual weight of the parcel. Carriers calculate a parcel's dimensional weight when it has a large size-to-weight ratio and compares actual weight to the dimensional weight. The larger weight is used to calculate the shipping rate. The following steps illustrate how to calculate cubic size and dimensional weight:

Determining the Cubic Size of a Parcel. The cubic size of a parcel is determined by multiplying height (inches) by length (inches) by width (inches) and rounding measurement to the nearest whole inch. Resulting total is the cubic size of the parcel (see Figure 23). Cubic size of multiple parcels are added together to determine the total shipment weight.

Figure 23: Cubic Size Calculations

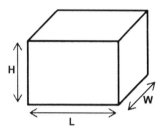

Domestic Shipments
Dimensional Weight (lbs) = (L x W x H) /194
L = Length in inches
W = Width in inches
H = Height in inches

International Shipments
Dimensional Weight (lbs) = (L x W x H) /166
L = Length in inches
W = Width in inches
H = Height in inches

Source: Adapted from UPS web site, "Dimensional Weight", http://www.ups.com/using/services/packing/dimwt-guide.html, accessed March 2003.

Calculating Weight (Domestic Shipments). Carriers use dimensional weight to bill a shipment when a parcel measures more than one cubic foot (1,728 inches). Actual weight is used to calculate the rate when cubic size is less than 1,728 inches. When the cubic size is greater than 1,728 inches, divide cubic size by 194 to determine dimensional weight in pounds.

Calculating Weight (International Shipments). Dimensional weight is calculated by dividing the cubic size of the parcel (in inches) by 166. To calculate the dimensional weight, when shown in kilograms, divide the cubic size of the parcel by 6000.

3.6.3 SIZE MATTERS

Carriers apply an *oversize* accessorial charge when a parcel exceeds the maximum standard dimensions for weight, size, and density. See Appendix 7, Oversized Parcels. Often, carriers will apply an additional charge for "irregular" size parcels when shape is incompatible with automated high-speed sortation systems. Parcel carriers categorize oversized shipments as "Oversize 1," "Oversize 2," and "Oversize 3."[174] It is important to compare the size and dimensions of the item to its container and consider additional oversize cost versus risk of damage because of reduced packaging. Innovative packaging can eliminate an extra handling charge when shipping irregular-shaped parcels.

A cost-cutting strategy is to reduce the number of parcels shipped to the same address by consolidating them into a larger parcel. Rates that are the highest are those for lower weight parcels. It costs more to ship two ten-pound parcels than a twenty-pound parcel. Shippers should use caution when banding or strapping to create a heavier parcel. Some carriers charge extra for these shipments because they catch on conveyors and the strapping can break. An alternative is to ship parcels in a sturdy master carton if the cost is less than the additional charge for loose parcels. See Appendix 8, Shipping Zone Rates, for an illustration of this concept.

3.7 Shipment Consolidation[175]

Shipment consolidation involves the practice of aggregating two or more small shipments into a single shipment, which reduces the cost of transportation. Generally, as shipment size increases, transportation costs will decrease. Such economies of density result from the effect shipment size, weight, and pieces have on a carrier's operating costs and rate structures. Consolidation involves aggregating customer orders across time and place. Aggregation across time occurs when shippers hold orders or delay purchases to consolidate shipments. Aggregation across place involves consolidating shipments to different destination within the same general area. Shippers may "pool" their orders to create larger shipments. A pooled shipment will move as a single consignment to a break-bulk facility such as a warehouse, distribution center, or carrier terminal. The role of a break-bulk facility is to separate shipments and deliver them to each individual customer. Opportunity to aggregate across place can be achieved in several ways by:

- using an intermediate breakbulk facility,
- using stop-off services, and
- pooling the traffic of different shippers.

When possible, shippers should look for a way to consolidate their shipments.[176] Shipping parcels on pallets is more cost-effective than shipping individual parcels. Combining multiple orders into a single parcel, banding boxes together, and palletizing shipments help reduce shipping costs. Airfreight shippers and international shippers take advantage of pricing strategies by placing multiple parcels on the same invoice or by negotiating rates that are based on a shipment's total weight instead of individual box weight.

3.8 Loss, Damage, and Delay Claims[177]

A claim against a carrier is a legal demand for payment of money arising from breach of the contract of carriage. Carriers' tariffs or their bills of lading, or both, outline their claim rules and govern their claims liability. International treaties govern export shipment. Court decisions interpret these regulations, laws, and tariffs, and determine the rights and obligations of the parties. For additional reference see National Motor Freight Classification (NMFC) Items regarding: (1) Principles and Practices for the Investigation and Disposition of Freight Claims, and (2) Regulations Governing the Inspection of Freight before or after Delivery to Consignee and Adjustment of Claims for Loss or Damage. There is no specific claim form prescribed by law, but four elements are essential: shipment identification, loss or damage description, amount of claim, and a demand for payment.[178]

Shipment Identification. Identify the shipment so the carrier can investigate the claim. Identification should include carrier's pro number, shipper's number, vehicle number, shipment date, delivery date, and commodity description.

Loss or Damage Description. A detailed description of the loss, damage, or delay should state (1) specific commodities, (2) type and number of units, (3) extent of loss suffered, (4) value of each unit, (5) amount of salvage realized, (6) net loss, and (7) a description of the events which caused the loss. Example:

10 cartons clothing – water damage @ $150.00 ea. = $1,500.00
2 cartons shoes short @ $350.00 ea. = $700.00
3 cartons china crushed @ $125.00 ea. = $375.00
$2,575.00 less $425.00 Salvage
Amount of Claim = $2,150.00

Note: See exception notation on the delivery receipt dated _____, confirmed by enclosed inspection report, dated _____.

Amount of claim. Claim should clearly state claimant's loss and include information on who is liable for the freight damage.[179] The claimant should place the carrier on notice regarding the potential loss liability exposure when damage amount is unknown.

A Demand for Payment. Submit the claim before the filing deadline, which is usually nine months from delivery, or the time prescribed by law. The date the carrier receives the claim determines if it has met the deadline. File a claim using a delivery method, which provides a confirmation of receipt. Receipt of claim by the delivering carrier is notice to all connecting carriers as well.

3.8.1 TYPES OF DAMAGE

There are two basic types of loss or damage—visible or noted loss or damage and concealed loss or damage.

Visible or Noted Loss or Damage. Visible loss or damage means the loss or damage was apparent at delivery. *Noted* means the carrier's delivery receipt gives a detailed description of the loss or damage.

Concealed Loss or Damage.[180] Concealed loss or damage simply means the loss or damage was not noticeable at delivery. The National Motor Freight Classification lists consignee and carrier obligations related to determining liability. Consider the following factors when determining liability in a concealed damage claim:

- Nature of goods
- Adequacy of packaging
- Movement before pickup or after delivery
- Condition of shipping containers

In a concealed damage claim, the consignee has the burden of proof. He or she must prove the carrier, not other parties who handled the goods, caused the damage.

3.8.2 RESPONSIBILITIES

A number of variables can affect a shipment during transport, such as (1) the number, size, and shape of other shipments traveling with it; (2) road conditions; (3) the weather; (4) warehousing conditions; and (5) special loading and handling requirements. To prevent or minimize loss and damage, consider all possible variables when designing a product, its packaging, and package markings.

Shipper's Responsibility. Shippers are responsible for proper packaging, which includes labels and markings. Shippers must provide a full commodity description on shipping papers and adhere to governing tariffs and regulations. The following publications state minimum packaging requirements.

- National Motor Freight Classification
- Hazardous Materials Regulations of the Department of Transportation

National Motor Freight Classification, Item 580, provides rules for proper marking, labeling, and tagging of freight. Item 680 of the same publication contains rules for packing and packaging. If Hazardous Materials Regulations of the Department of Transportation govern the shipment, Items 580 and 680 do not apply.

Carrier's Responsibility. Carriers have the responsibility to deliver a shipment in the same condition received. Carriers must compensate for losses or damages they cause, subject to terms and conditions outlined in the bill of lading and carrier tariffs. Limited liability will apply if a shipment moves under a release value or contract carriage. However, shippers can purchase additional liability insurance from carriers by requesting it on the bill of lading, or from a third-party insurer. Shipments moving out of Canada or Mexico are subject to a different liability than domestic shipments.

Carrier must *acknowledge* a claim in writing within thirty days after receipt and provide the claimant a claim number.[181] The carrier will pay, refuse payment, or make a compromise offer within 120 days after receipt. Carriers will notify claimants when they are unable to settle their claim within 120 days. Carriers are required to keep claimants informed at sixty-day intervals until the claim is settled.

Carriers will *inspect* shipment within five normal workdays after receipt of a request from a consignee.[182] Inspection will include examination of the damaged merchandise, shipping container, and any other action necessary to establish the facts. A carrier submits an original copy of findings to consignee for their claim support. If a carrier fails to inspect the shipment, the consignee must do so and record all information.[183]

Consignee's Responsibility. A consignee must identify and document loss and damage on the delivery receipt at the time of delivery. General terms, such as "box damaged," to describe damage should not be used. Vague descriptions do not provide adequate support for a claim. Instead, use specific details, such as "release handle broken" or "6-inch scratch on framework," to describe the extent of damage. At delivery, a consignee must:

- check each handling unit for signs of damage,
- open any shipments that show signs of loss or damage in the presence of the driver, and
- examine contents with the driver.

It is important to have the driver sign the consignee's copy of the delivery receipt. It may be more difficult to obtain prompt and satisfactory settlement of a claim if the delivery receipt does not state the damage. Record a detailed description of results on all copies of the delivery receipt. Regarding concealed loss or damage, the consignee must notify the carrier immediately in writing and keep the shipment (containers and contents) in the same condition in which it arrived.

Shortages. The consignee must check for shortages at delivery. Check the labels on all handling units and count the actual number of units. The consignee should make a written tally record when there are numerous items or the shipment comprises many different items. Keep the shipment together until unloading is complete, in case a recount is necessary. If there is a shortage, describe it in precise terms on both carrier and consignee copies of the delivery receipt, before signing for the shipment.

Mitigation of Loss. The consignee cannot refuse to accept a shipment just because of damage or partial loss. The consignee must accept and act to minimize the loss. It is then appropriate to file a claim for depreciation, repair costs, or replacement of loss goods.

Salvage. The owner of a shipment (consignee) must minimize their loss.[184] The consignee can reduce loss by selling damaged freight at a discounted price or having damaged goods repaired. Reducing loss will often expedite a claim settlement. If the shipment is a total loss, consult the carrier for disposition instructions.

NOTE: Courts have ruled that a consignee many not open a container and examine the merchandise before giving a receipt to the carrier unless there is visual indication of probable internal damage.

3.8.3 FILING LOSS AND DAMAGE CLAIM

Only shippers, consignees, or a third party who has claim or title to a shipment may file a claim. A claim is filed with the carrier on whose line the loss or damage occurred. Regarding time limits, a bill of lading contract specifies the carrier must receive claim within nine months after delivery of shipment. Deadline for a "failure to deliver" claim is nine months after a reasonable time for delivery has elapsed. Following are basic documentation required to support a claim.[185]

- Description of damage or loss
- Calculations to support claim amount
- Bill of lading or consignee copy of delivery receipt
- Vendor invoice for the goods
- Invoice for repaired goods

3.8.4 OVERCHARGE CLAIM

Carriers must collect no more or no less than the legitimate freight charge. If determined that a carrier has overcharged for a shipment, the payer of the invoice or their agent must submit supporting documentation to recover the excess charges. Typical documentation requirements are:

- original or certified copy of the invoice;
- certified copy of original invoice for a claim based on weight, valuation, or incorrect commodity description;
- original bill of lading for misrouting or valuation claim; and
- weight certificate or certified statement for a weight claim.

3.8.5 SUIT DEADLINE

If a carrier denies liability for a loss, for which the claimant has reason to believe the carrier is lawfully liable, the claimant has the right to institute a lawsuit. The lawsuit must originate within the established time limit. The most commonly applicable suit time limit is two years and one day from the date the carrier disallowed the claim. The mailing date of the carrier's disallowance letter usually governs, not the date letter was received by the claimant. The "Carmack Amendment" governs truck traffic (49 U.S.C 14706) and rail traffic (49 U.S.C. 11706). Not all traffic is subject to the Carmack Amendment. A written statement declining payment of a claim in full or in part begins the deadline for filing suit. The claimant should periodically review the status of a pending claim to prevent missing the suit filing deadline.

Partners in transportation have a direct interest in loss and damage and have an exposure to liability. Claims filed require the transportation industry to pay out billions of dollars annually. Indirect costs amount to many times the actual damages. Indirect costs arise from claims administration, insurance premiums, replacement costs, capital tied up in claims proceedings, and customer dissatisfaction. For example, if a company is operating at a 2 percent operating ratio, it would take $50,000 in sales to offset a $1,000 freight loss ($1,000 / 2%). Table 13 illustrates the cost of claims based on different operating ratios.

Table 13: What Freight Loss and Damage Really Cost

OPERATING RATIO (%)	DAMAGE OR LOSS CLAIM						
	$50	$100	$200	$300	$400	$500	$1,000
	EQUALS SALES OF						
1%	$5,000	$10,000	$20,000	$30,000	$40,000	$50,000	$100,000
2%	$2,500	$5,000	$10,000	$15,000	$20,000	$25,000	**$50,000**
3%	$1,667	$3,333	$6,667	$10,000	$13,333	$16,667	$33,383
4%	$1,250	$2,500	$5,000	$7,500	$10,000	$12,500	$25,000

Source: Based on Institute of Logistics Management, "Freight Claims Management," http://www.logistics-edu.com/course_freightclaims.html, accessed July 2004.

A strong partnership between all parties—shipper, vendors, and carriers—will help minimize risk for all involved parties.[186] With everyone working in harmony, the process of packaging, shipping, and receiving becomes more efficient. Companies should develop a claim prevention program and provide training to employees. Shipping managers should consistently check on their vendors to insure they follow proper packaging and labeling procedures. On the inbound receiving side, trained employees should inspect freight and compare shipments to applicable shipping documents before signing the delivery receipt. Train employees to recognize and follow special handling instructions when unpacking, moving and storing freight.

3.9 Contracting[187]

A *contract* is a written representation of the negotiations and deliberations of two or more parties. In traffic management, the term *contracting* refers to tasks, skills, and activities necessary to build and maintain alliances to acquire transportation services. To create effective agreements, managers must have knowledge of contracting methods, contract law, cost estimating techniques, good negotiating skills, and contract terminology. Because of their complex nature, written agreements form a more definitive record and reference than does a verbal contract. Being able to refer to a document is mutually beneficial. Contracts should be concise and easily understood by all concerned parties. See Appendix 9, Contract Terminology.

Why Contract? Background research leads up to a decision about which method for purchasing transportation services is best for the company.[188] For contracting to work, each party should gain something. The carrier expects a commitment of traffic that assures freight revenue contributes to its profitability and supports its strategic planning. Carriers rely on short-term contracts as a flexible instrument that permits rapid adjustments to changing market conditions. For shippers, contracting can lead to lower rates and the flexibility to mold services to fit the company. Contracting can benefit shippers in the following ways:

1. Lower rates. A reduced rate is the single most important reason for contracting. A shipper's negotiating advantage and potential rate reduction often depends on the size and term of its commitment.
2. Fewer tariffs to support. If a shipper and its carriers can agree to rules and rate automation, there is a diminished need for manual tariffs.
3. Better information exchange. A shipper-carrier contract can create a favorable environment for utilizing technology. Electronic transmission of shipping documents and other correspondence will lower costs while improving productivity.
4. Greater Control. Contract agreement with a limited number of carriers will lessen the shipper's monitoring requirements.

5. Confidentially. Because shippers do not have to publicize any competitive advantage gained by bargaining, many view confidentiality as an important feature of contracting.
6. Design flexibility. Contracting affords shippers flexibility in designing contract terms and conditions to address their needs.

For both shipper and carrier, contracting can be instrumental in helping to create a stronger alliance. Shipper and carrier are able to discard any adversary relationship that may exist and form a relationship that can benefit both parties by contributing to technological and productivity improvements. Shippers should monitor contract performance compliance, which begins after the contract takes effect. Contracts should be clear and concise to (1) minimize disputes (2) provide the parties with a specific set of rules, and (3) assure all parties that expectations are achievable.

3.9.1 HISTORICAL OVERVIEW

To describe motor carriage today clearly resembles the description used in the past, but the legal structure that surrounded that description no longer exists. The ICC Termination Act of 1995 eliminated the Interstate Commerce Commission and placed transportation regulation under the Surface Transportation Board (STB) of the Department of Transportation. Deregulation eliminated the distinction between common and contract motor carriers. However, use of the terms continues within the industry. Between August 9, 1935, and January 1, 1995, there were three forms of freight motor carriage recognized in law:[189]

Common Carriage is defined as carriers who hold themselves out to the public to perform transportation and related services. The Interstate Commerce Commission and various state regulatory agencies issued such authority.

Contract Carriage, defined as a for-hire carrier, does not hold itself out to service the public, but instead services a limited number of shippers. This contract requires the carrier to provide a specified transportation service at a specified cost.

Private Carriage is defined as performing transportation services *"in the furtherance of the primary business enterprise."* An example would be a manufacturer that transports its product in company-registered equipment and whose drivers are under the manufacturer's control. Private carriers own or lease transportation equipment and operate their own facilities.

There are two distinct types of contracts recognize by professionals in the transportation industry. The *Bill of Lading is* a contract for carriage and addresses a "single shipment." Contract carriage agreements cover multiple shipments and create a long-term or "continuing contract." These two contracts serve different purposes and are not interchangeable.

3.9.2 SHIPPER'S PROFILE

Negotiating for contract services is essentially the same as negotiating for any other service. The initial approach begins with understanding what services are required to support the company and customer demands and then compiling the information into a "Transportation Purchasing Profile."[190] The profile should describe the company's underlying philosophy, how to purchase required services, and parameters used for carrier selection. Often, shippers and carriers do not act in concert because of differences in perception, practice, or philosophy. This can impede cooperation and result in conflict between shipper and carrier. An important first step is for shippers to understand how carriers view their business.

Understanding your freight business. Understanding how carriers view a company's business and what shipping characteristics are important to the carrier are important. Carriers analyze a shipper's profile to determine if the freight is easy to handle, profitable, and will fit into their existing network. There are basic shipping characteristics that carriers look for in a client:

1. Parcel volume. This is important because it directly affects the carrier's pickup costs and ability to control costs.
2. Parcel weight and distance it must travel. Heavier parcels and longer travel distance are good characteristics for carriers because heavy parcels and longer distance mean more revenue.
3. Delivery costs. Residential deliveries are more costly to the carrier because typically they only involve one parcel. Generally, commercial stops involve multiple parcels within a short distance compared with residential deliveries where stops are over a much larger area.

Parcel characteristics are a key factor used in the carrier's price-making process. Other considerations include claims ratio, accounts payable, oversize parcels, and hazardous and dangerous material parcels. Shippers' awareness of these characteristics and their impact on a carrier's operating costs will better prepare them for the negotiation process. A shipper with a desirable shipping profile will have an advantage when negotiating a transportation agreement. The more a shipper can help control a carrier's delivery cost, the more bargaining power it will have during the negotiation process.

Identify Your Shipping Needs. Identifying shipping needs and articulating them will help insure the carrier's service is consistent with the shipper's transportation profile. While there are similarities among firms, there are distinct differences in performance requirements. Identify present and future shipping needs before negotiating for delivery services. A company should conduct a transportation audit to support its strategic planning. It may be not all customers require the same service. Provide carriers with information such as products shipped, destinations shipped to, special handling characteristics, and service expectations.[191]

A contract program can be complex, labor intensive, and expensive. The need for sound negotiating, costing, and basic legal skills can impose additional training and educational requirements. After signing the contract, shippers should administer changes, contingency clauses, performance compliance, renewal, or termination. The cost and complexity of contracting require constant monitoring of contract compliance and carrier performance. See Appendix 10, Contracting Cycle.

3.9.3 WHAT CONTRACTING METHOD?

Once management decides to contract, it must then make a choice of what contracting method to use. When deciding whether to use a *competitive bidding* method or a *negotiation contract* method, companies often attempt to forecast transaction costs under each method. Selecting the appropriate contract type and managing it effectively will help improve the quality of the company's overall logistics function. In addition, it will serve to reduce conflicts between shippers and carriers. Following is a discussion of two basic contracting methods used in the parcel delivery industry.

Competitive Bidding. This approach requires shippers to solicit competitive bids for well-defined transportation services and, with everything being equal, award the lowest bidder. Ordinarily, the bid represents a carrier's rate for services rendered. The bidding process is most effective when all parties understand what services are required. With this contracting method, shipper must allow sufficient time for carriers to view bid advertisement and to submit bids. The following conditions frequently produce good results:

1. Suitable traffic. Shipping volume and the nature of traffic must establish sufficient incentive for carriers to offer a competitive rate-service package. Other favorable traffic characteristics add incentives by allowing the carrier to cut operating costs.
2. Adequate competition. In practice, a minimum of two carriers may provide adequate competition, but more bidders will make the process more competitive. The pool of potential bidders should comprise only carriers that can meet the shipper's transportation service requirements.
3. Sufficient time to prepare. Contracting frequently requires considerable background research and preparation. An initial contracting program may require many months to implement.

An advantage of competitive bidding is the ability to gather bids from a larger group of carriers than under the negotiation method. Negotiating for services is a more costly activity than simply preparing and submitting a bid package. Because a larger number of companies participate in competitive bidding, shippers are more likely to find carriers willing to offer favorable rates using this method. A disadvantage of competitive bidding is that carriers often inflate their bids for unspecified contingencies when the shipper's service requirements are vague. Service requirements that are clear and unchanged throughout the contract period make the bid method more effective. For competitive reasons, requirements should not be overly restrictive.

Negotiation method. Negotiating is discussion, bargaining, and compromise to the mutual benefit of all parties. The exact nature of the contract evolves from negotiations in which all aspects of rates and services are eligible for discussion. The negotiation method offers a flexible approach that identifies problems and explores service requirements.[192] The negotiation method is frequently preferred when the following conditions arise:

1. Traffic uncertainty. Negotiation method offers opportunity for shippers and carriers to examine and discuss economic adjustments and contingencies.
2. Significant change in carrier operations. If a carrier must alter its operations to meet a shipper's needs, all parties should analyze and discuss current and future relations and services requirements.
3. Available cost data. While there can be drastic and unpredictable fluctuations in rate determinants, experienced shippers will have a reasonably good idea of an acceptable range of rates. Cost data is necessary to arrive at an accurate estimate of a carrier's unit costs and evaluate proposed rates.

There are people in the freight transportation industry that feel the negotiation process has some distinct advantages versus competitive bidding. First, shippers can reduce delay by requesting carriers immediately prepare their bids. Second, since the negotiation process normally involves a smaller group of carriers, it can provide shippers a higher degree of privacy. Third, it is felt that shippers have a greater chance of selecting a reputable carrier when using the negotiation process.

3.9.4 SOURCING

Sourcing is the process of identifying and selecting qualified sources of supply. The sourcing process plays a key role in transportation contracting because a shipper's key objective is to identify a group of carriers who have the capability, desire, and commitment to meet shipper's needs. After compiling a list of potential carriers, shippers should screen the list to identify the most qualified carriers. This process involves two basic issues: screening potential carriers and how many carriers.

Screening carriers. It is important for shippers to evaluate the strength and weaknesses of carriers to ensure they are qualified to participate in the contracting process. Carriers qualified to participate will possess the required operational and financial capability, as well as business integrity, to meet shipper's transportation needs. Traffic levels, complexity and duration of the contract, and knowledge or experience with carriers are major factors that will impact the shipper's evaluation process. Shippers should evaluate three key aspects of the carrier's business:

- Operational capability
- Financial capability
- Management capability and orientation

Carriers selected should have the capacity to service a shipper's transportation needs.[193] It is important to select a financially viable partner. Financially weak carriers can pose a risk if they are not able to invest in their business and perform quality service. Carrier's management should exhibit a clear record of sound business integrity. Shippers need to feel confident in a carrier's degree of commitment to the letter and spirit of the contract.

How many carriers?[194] Studies have shown that dealing with fewer carriers can reduce a shipper's administrative load and carrier management cost, while capitalizing on basic transportation economics—trading increased volume for lower rates. Industry professionals recommend shippers implement a core carrier program and concentrate shipments to a select number of capable, high-performance carriers. Shippers should guarantee carriers a portion of projected volume in return for lower rates and a higher service commitment. Shippers should leverage their total *freight buy* and turn carriers into partners who are committed to improving service and lowering transportation cost.

3.9.5 NOTIFICATION

Today's traffic managers fully recognize the need to select carriers based on a thorough evaluation of rates and service, as well as a carrier's ability to meet their company's needs. To facilitate the selection process, shippers often issue a bid document called a Request for Proposals (RFPs) to identify finalists. The objective of the competitive bidding process is to qualify only carriers who have the necessary financial expertise, management capability, and experience for executing and operating a project efficiently.

Evaluate requirements and conduct a formalized RFP process. A shipper's process should measure a carrier's attributes, such as on-time performance, acceptance rates, type of equipment, and equipment availability. It is important to present requirements in a clear and concise manner. An RFP that is full of unnecessary detail and requests for irrelevant information can discourage carriers and is counterproductive. RFPs should include bidding requirements—presentation requirement, deadline for solicitation and submission, carrier evaluation and selection procedures, contracting procedures, and rates and terms negotiation. Include in the RFP the notification process regarding carrier selection or rejection.

What to include in an RFP. It is a delicate balance to write an RFP that is not long and burdensome, but also not so vague to be meaningless. It is important to know if solicited carriers have the ability to back up their promises, and how a shipper's profile will fit into the carrier's business plan. An RFP provides standards for carrier proposals and highlights the business, technical, and legal issues to be included in the final contract.[195]

An RFP's language and format can adversely affect the accuracy and timely submission of a carrier's response. The document should be concise and in a format that is easy to follow and complete. Clearly state the evaluation and weighting factors that will be used to score the proposal. Allow sufficient time for carriers to prepare a good proposal. Clarify to all concerned the method that will be used to benchmarked or score RFPs. Finally, have people with knowledge of the transportation industry and the company's needs review RFPs for content and clarity.

3.9.6 EVALUATION AND AWARD

When awarding a contract, a properly structured RFP process will provide a shipper an opportunity to consider the full range of services offered by responsive carriers. During the *competitive bid* process, it is important to eliminate *unresponsive* bids or isolate them for corrective action. *Responsive* bids are those that meet the deadline and specifications and are free of mistakes. The evaluation process should be *transparent* in that it allows an objective third party to verify the fairness of an award decision. Shippers often find that carriers show a wide variation of strengths and weaknesses. Since the lowest bidder may not always produce the best results, shippers should judge bids on alternative-rate-service combinations. A typical approach is to list specific service attributes and assign a value that reflects their relative importance to the company. A shipper's objective analysis should include the *cost of service*. Subjective business judgments, as well as rigorous quantitative analyses, should be applied to carriers who have similar ranking.

Responsiveness, as defined for competitive bidding, is not an issue in the negotiation method. Here, the goal is to promote flexibility and encourage discussion of alternative solutions. Initially, the shipper will present to carriers its transportation service requirements. A presentation typically covers all the basic elements, including traffic and lane volumes, expected service levels, equipment requirements, and costs. Typically, negotiations follow the presentation and continue until a general agreement is reached on the key elements. Generally, one party will take responsibility for preparing the initial draft contract that address issues such as, credit, billing, payment reports, liability, claims, penalties, default, termination, or renewal. A key objective of the contract award process is to ensure carriers proposals are responsive to the shipper's needs and objectively evaluated, and that contracts are awarded fairly. When it comes time to award a contract, most likely the best choice will be the carrier who offers the best rates and services. There should be a good fit between the shipper's requirements and carrier's capabilities. Without proper awarding practices, there is little assurance the selected carrier is the most qualified at the best price.

Automated RFP Process. Automating RFP creation and evaluation is an ideal way to ensure fairness for carriers involved in the bidding process. Automation allows shippers to build an RFP on standardized templates and creates a single, centralized repository for storing data. Most importantly, automation takes much of the subjectivity out of comparing and judging bids. Bid-solutions remove subjective interpretations by automatically pulling data from electronically transmitted proposals and inserting data into predetermined fields in a comparison matrix. Solutions that integrate bidding, contracting, and transportation management make it possible to update information, business rules, and evaluate carriers' performance.

3.9.7 CONTRACT ADMINISTRATION

Contract administration involves activities performed after a contract is awarded. The purpose is to determine how well the carrier is meeting contract requirements.[196] These activities constitute the primary part of the procurement process that insures compliance. Factors influencing the degree of contract administration include the nature of work, experience, and commitment of personnel involved. Contract administration starts with developing a clear and concise performance-based statement of service and a plan that effectively measures carrier's service performance.[197] Contract monitoring is essential in identifying and resolving any problem that may arise. Contracts should be monitored to ensure carriers are complying with contract terms and achieving performance expectations. Without a sound monitoring process, there is no assurance a shipper is receiving what the contract calls for.

To insure customer satisfaction, shippers should seek direct input from their customers through a customer satisfaction survey. A carefully constructed survey can provide valuable feedback concerning shipper and carrier performance. The survey also serves as tool to help determine subsequent contract awards. Good contract administration enhances shipper, carrier, and customer satisfaction.

SECTION IV – APPENDICES

1. Typical Parcel Movement from Origin to Destination
2. Key Financials (2009 & 2010)
3. Exterior Packaging Materials
4. Comparative Securing Systems
5. How to Read UN Markings
6. Parcel Delivery Providers
7. Oversize Parcels
8. Shipping Zone Rates
9. Contract Terminology
10. Contracting Cycle

APPENDIX 1: Typical Parcel Movement from Origin to Destination

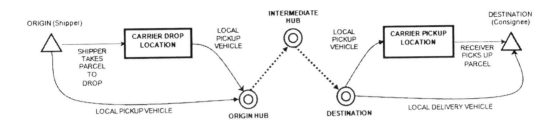

·········▶ Parcels Move Line-haul (over-the-road truck or via rail or air) Between Hubs

Source: Based on, Edward K. Morlok, Bradley F. Nitzberg, Karthik Balasubramaniam and Mark L. Sand, The Parcel Service Industry in the U.S.: Its size and Role In Commerce, Systems Engineering Department, University of Pennsylvania, (2000), Figure 1, p.6.

APPENDIX 2: Key Financials (2009 & 2010)

	United Parcel Service (UPS)[1]		FedEx Corporation (FedEx)[2]		United States Parcel Service (USPS)[3]	
Fiscal Year – End	Dec 09	Dec 10	May 09	May 10	Sept 09	Sept 10
Revenue (Millions)	$45,297.0	$49,545.0	$35,497.0	$34,784.0	$68,090.0	$67,050.0
Net Income (Millions)	$2,152.0	$3,488.0	$98.0	$1,184.0	($3,740.0)	($8,510.0)
Employees	408,000	400,600	280,000	141,000	596,000	583,908
Fortune 500 Ranking #	43	48	60	73	Not Applicable	

NOTE: FedEx reported revenue of $39,304.0 Million for fiscal year ending May 31, 2011.

Source: [1]Wikipedia, the free encyclopedia. United Parcel Service, Inc. http://en.wikipedia.org/wiki/United_Parcel_Service (05/21/2010 and 08/18/2011) and MSN Money. United States Parcel, Inc. http://moneycentral.msn.com/investor/invsub/results/statement.aspx?symbol=UPS (05/21/2010 and 08/18/2011).
[2]Wikipedia, the free encyclopedia. FedEx Corporation. http://en.wikipedia.org/wiki/FedEx (05/21/2010 and 08/18/2011) and MSN Money. FedEx Corporation. http://moneycentral.msn.com/investor/invsub/results/statement.aspx?symbol=fsx (05/21/2010 and 08/18/2011).
[3]Wikipedia, the free encyclopedia. http://en.wikipedia.org/wiki/United_States_Postal_Service (05/21/2010 and 08/18/2011)

APPENDIX 3: Exterior Packaging Materials

Type of Exterior Packaging	Stacking Strength / Crush Resistance	Cushioning Providing	Application
Corrugated Boxes	Good	No – must use cushioning material	It is estimated that corrugated boxes are used to ship over 95% of all products in the U.S.
Corrugated Mailers	Very Good	No – must use cushioning material	Books, tools, flat items such as pictures
Bubble Mailers	Poor	Yes	Products that require some cushioning but no stacking strength - CDs, DVDs, books, vitamins, dental & medical supplies
Padded Mailers	Poor	Yes	Products that require some cushioning but no stacking strength - CDs, DVDs, books, vitamins, dental & medical supplies
Tyvek Envelopes	Poor	No – must use cushioning material	Non-fragile items such as printed catalogs and documents, clothing, tools
Stay Flat Mailers	Good	No – must use cushioning material	Items that cannot be bent, such as documents, CDs and DVDs, photographs, posters
Courier Envelopes	Poor	No – must use cushioning material	Non-fragile items such as printed catalogs and documents, clothing, tools
Mailing Tubes	Good	No – must use cushioning material	Posters, blueprints, artwork, wedding invitations, diplomas and calendars
Wooden Crates	Excellent	No – must use cushioning material	Low volume, heavy and fragile items such as vehicle engines, glass chandeliers, original oil paintings and telecommunications equipment
Plastic Cases	Good	No – must use cushioning material	Medical and musical instruments

Source: Based on PackagingPrice.com, "How do I package my product for shipping?," http//:www.packagingprice.com, accessed April 2008,

APPENDIX 4: Comparative Securing Systems

Closure System	Material	Dust Proof	Quick Sealing	Cost	Sensitive to Humidity	Adhesion to All Surfaces
Adhesive	Cold Glue	No	No	Low	Yes	No
Adhesive	Hot Glue	No	Yes	High	No	Yes
Tape	Gummed Kraft	Yes	Yes	Low	Yes	No
Tape	Reinforced Gummed Kraft	Yes	Yes	Medium	Yes	No
Tape	Pressure Sensitive	Yes	Yes	High	No	Yes
Stitching or Stapling	Metal	No	Yes	High	No	Yes
Strapping	Metal	No	Yes	Medium	No	Yes
Strapping	Plastic	No	Yes	Low	No	Yes

Source: Adapted from The Canadian Trade Commission Service, "A Guide for Exporters," 2000.

APPENDIX 5: How to Read UN Markings

How to Read ... Using the Drum as an example – <u>1A1 / X1.5 / 250 / 01</u>
<u>USA / M123</u>

UN Indicates United Nations approved packaging:

1. Type of Package

    1. Drums/Pails
    2. Barrels
    3. Jerricans
    4. Boxes
    5. Bags
    6. Composite Packaging

A. Material of Construction

    A. Steel
    B. Aluminum
    C. Wood
    D. Fibre
    E. Plastic

1. Category Within Type

    1. Closedhead
    2. Openhead

X.   Packaging Group for which drum was tested

   X. for Packaging Group I, II, III
   Y. for Packing Group I, and III
   Z. for Packing Group III
   Packaging Group I: Great Danger (high hazard level)
   Packaging Group II: Medium Danger (medium hazard level)
   Packaging Group III: Minor Danger (low hazard level)

1.5 The density or specific gravity marking indicates the drum is rated for liquids with a specific gravity of 1.5 or less.

OR

For packaging intended for solids, this marking will indicate the maximum gross mass (weight) in kilograms.

250 The hydraulic pressure rating in this example is 250 kilo-pascal (kPa).

OR

For packaging intended for solids, an "S" in uppercase will follow the gross mass.

[01]   Year container was manufactured

[USA]   Country where drum was manufactured

[M123]   Code for manufacturing plant

NOTE: UN markings stamped on a UN rated drum indicate it has been tested to meet the Performance Oriented Packaging (POP) standards outlined by the Department of Transportation at 49 Code of Federal Regulations (CFR) 178.

Source: Based on, Federal Motor Carrier Safety Administration, *Performance Oriented Package Marking*, http://www.fmcsa.dot.gov/safety-security/hazmat/complyhmregs.htm#hm, accessed December 2009.

APPENDIX 6: Parcel Delivery Providers

4 Couriers
Provides a network of web guides that helps users find information online
www.4 couriers.com

AAA Express
Provides same-day delivery service throughout the United States and Puerto Rico
www.aaaxfast.com

APX Worldwide Express
Provides international door-to-door air courier services
www.apr-air-courier.com

Bellair Express
Provides domestic and international airfreight forwarding services
www.bellair.com

Bravo Message Service
Full service message company
www.bravomessenger.com

CrossCountry Courier
Provides same-day and overnight delivery service to locations in the Midwest
www.deliveryconnection.com

Express Messenger Systems
Nationwide courier service with offices in nine cities
www.exmess.com

FedEx Online Shipping
Site allows users to schedule pickups, track packages, and locate drop off boxes.
www.fedex.com

Global Freight Systems
Provides next-day air and truck services throughout the U.S. and Canada
www.globalfreightsystems.com

Greyhound Package Express
Provides nationwide package delivery services to urban and rural communities
www.shipgreyhound.com

Hot Shot Express
Provider of courier services for expedited and dedicated-route deliveries
www.hsxp.com

iShip.com
Online marketplace that compares prices and services among shipping and mailing carriers
www.iship.com

Movefreight
Provider of ground transportation, airfreight, rail, and ocean transport services
www.movefreight.com

Overnite Express Parcel Service
Overnight parcel delivery service in Southern California
www.overniteexpress.com

Parcel Logistics
Provides trackable parcel delivery throughout the U.S., Canada, and Mexico
www.parcellogistics.com

Parcel Logistics
Provides traceable small parcel delivery throughout the U.S., Canada, and Mexico
www.parcellogistics.com

Parcel Plus
Drop-off center for FedEx and UPS packages
www.parcelplus.com

The Mail Bank
Drop-off location for Federal Express, UPS, TNT, and USPS Services

Saturn Freight Systems
Provides air service, express LTL, economy TL, and exclusive truck service
www.saturnfreight.com

SkyNet Courier
Provides delivery of time-sensitive documents to worldwide destinations
www.skynetmia.com

SkyPak
Providers of courier services worldwide
www.skypak.com

Supplier Inspection Services
Provider of on-site sorting and controlled shipping services

Symplex Courier Systems
Provides "on-demand scheduled" pickup for small parcels and packages
www.symplexcourier.com

U.S. Postal Service (USPS) Priority Mail
Small parcel and letter delivery service
www.uspsprioritymail.com

Ultra Ex
Nationwide logistics company offering same-day and overnight services
www.ultraex.com

United Parcel Service
Provides specialized transportation and logistics services and package delivery
www.ups.com

Vital Express
Nationwide logistics company offering logistics services including messenger services
www.vitalexpress.com

Xmessenger
Guide to same-day domestic shipping of packages and a database of airports and couriers
www.xmessenger.com

Source: Listing compiled from various sources such as, b2bYellowpages.com, "B2B Transportation Directory," http://www.b2byellowpages.com/directory/b2b_transportation/small-package-delivery.shtml, accessed June 2010.

APPENDIX 7: Oversize Parcels

SERVICES	UPS	FedEx Express Ground	FedEx Home Delivery
Additional Handling	$6.00	$6.00	$6.00
Additional Handling Application	over 60 in. length	over 60 in. length	over 60 in. length
Air Dimensional Factor (Domestic)	L x W x H/194	L x W x H/194	N/A
Air Dimensional Weight Minimum (Domestic)	no minimum size	no minimum size	N/A
Maximum Length	108 in.	119 in. air/108 in. ground	108 in.
Maximum Length + Girth	165 in.	165 in.	130 in.
Maximum Weight	150 lbs.	150 lbs.	70 lbs.
Ground Oversize 1 Charge (84 in. L + G)	30 lbs.	30 lbs.	30 lbs.
Ground Oversize 2 Charge (>108 in. <130 in. L + G)	70 lbs.	50 lbs.	50 lbs.
Ground Oversize 3 Charge (>130 in. <165 in. L + G)	90 lbs. minimum + Surcharge	90 lbs. minimum + Surcharge	90 lbs. minimum + Surcharge
Large Air Package (>130 in. <165 in. L + G)	90 lbs. minimum + Surcharge	90 lbs. minimum + Surcharge	N/A

Source: Data compiled from UPS and FedEx websites, accessed 2006.

APPENDIX 8: Shipping Zone Rates

Shippers need to know what they are shipping (weight and dimensions), where they are shipping (destination zone), and what carrier services they want to use. Parcel carriers publish zone charts, which identify distance codes referred to as "zones." Zone charts create a matrix of originating and designating ZIP codes and identifies the correct zone for the designated distance. To view or printout a zone chart specific to the origin zone, a shipper enters the origin ZIP code into a zone locator. The zone locator chart lists a zone for any shipment sent within the United States. USPS, for example, designates its distance zones as "local" and "1 through 8."

Extracted from zone chart created for shipments originating in ZIP Codes: 21000-21299

Destination ZIP	Zone
156	3
157	2
158	3
159	2
160-165	3
166	2
167	3
168	2
169	3
170-187	2
188	3
189-232	2

Determining Shipping Costs

Step 1: To create a zone chart specific to an origin location, enter origin ZIP into a carrier's zone locator. For example, ZIP code 21244 is the origin ZIP used to create a zone chart, using FedEx zone locator.

Step 2: To determine the destination zone, take the first three digits of the destination ZIP code (17268) and refer to the zone chart. For example, ZIP code 17268 is in Zone 2.

Step 3: Knowing the destination zone allows shippers to view or print a table showing rates by various services and weights for a shipment's destination zone within the U.S.

Quantity of packages is important in determining a shipment's delivery charge. Opportunities to lower shipping charges exist when combining packages. For example, two five-pound packages shipped from zip code 21244 to zip code 17268 (FedEx First Overnight) cost $27.90 each or $55.80 total. Combining the two packages into one ten-pound package lowers the charge for the same service to $30.65, a savings of $25.15.

FedEx Express – Domestic Services

Domestic Rates: Zone 2			
Weight (Lb.)	FedEx First Overnight	FedEx Priority Overnight	FedEx 2-Day
1	27.90	15.30	14.70
2	27.90	15.30	14.70
3	27.90	15.30	14.70
4	27.90	15.30	14.70
5	27.90	15.30	14.70
6	28.45	15.50	14.90
...			
10	30.65	16.30	15.70

Source: Data Extracted from FedEx Web Site, www.fedex.com/us/rates, rates in effect January 2, 2006

NOTE: The objective of this appendix is to illustrate the use of a carrier's website to create a zone chart and rate table. Carrier rates are subject to change and should always be verified.

APPENDIX 9: Contract Terminology

A thorough knowledge of contract *terms* (or definitions) encountered when contracting for goods and services allows a better understanding of the contract. The following contract terminology is common within the parcel delivery industry.

Accessorial Charge – Charge applied to the cost of a shipment for various reasons, such as oversize, address or bill of lading correction, and residential delivery.

Addendum – Addition or supplement to a solicitation document.

Advertise – Public announcement of an intent to purchase goods and services.

Awardee – Person or entity approved for a contract.

Bid – Document submitted in response to a bid solicitation to provide goods and services under specific terms and conditions.

Bid Bond – Written agreement that guarantees a bidder will accept a contract as bid, if awarded.

Bid Deposit – Money or check deposited that guarantees a bidder will accept the contract as bid, if awarded.

Bidder – Person or business that submits a bid in response to a bid solicitation.

Bidders List – List of vendor names and addresses who have expressed interest in providing goods and services.

Bid Opening – Public opening to read and record the names of bidders responding to a bid solicitation.

Bid Solicitation – Document that requests submittal of bids for goods or services.

Bid Tabulation – Recording of bids submitted in response to a bid solicitation for purposes of comparison, analysis, and record keeping.

Cell-by-cell Pricing – Pricing formula used to determine the rate for a specific weight and zone combination.

Commodity – Article of trade or commerce made available for sale or barter.

Competitive Sealed Bidding – Process of publicizing an invitation of bids, conducting public bid openings, and awarding a contract.

Contract – Formal agreement executed by two or more parties.

Contractor – Person or entity awarded a contract.

Delivery Codes – Code used to classify delivery destinations as rural or urban.

Delivery Density – Volume of items such as parcels and letters delivered at one time to one address.

Evaluation of Bids and Proposals – Process used to determine a bidder's responsiveness to contract requirements.

Insurance – A contract that protects the insured against loss or damage, accident, or death.

Joint Venture – Contractual agreement entered into by two or more persons or entities for a common benefit.

Legal Notice – Public notice required by law.

Letter of Credit – Document issued by a bank, which authorizes the bearer to draw money from an account.

Lowest Responsive and Responsible Bidder – Bidder with the lowest price, who prepared and submitted required documents under a bid solicitation and who is able to perform and deliver under specified terms.

Matrix Pricing – Pricing based on discounts that may change for each service, depending upon weight or zone.

Net Minimum Rate – A set rate or gross cost of a one-pound zone 2 package, that ensures the carrier a minimum revenue for making a delivery.

No Bid – Response to an invitation for bids stating the bidder does not wish to submit an offer. It usually operates as a procedural consideration to prevent suspension from the bidders' list for failure to submit bids.

Nonresponsive Bids – A bid that does not conform to mandatory requirements of a solicitation.

Payment and Performance – Bond executed under a contract that secures the payment and performance requirements of a bidder and fulfillment of all undertakings, terms, conditions, and agreements contained in a contract.

Person – An individual, corporation, partnership, joint venture, association, unincorporated association, trust, or other legal entity.

Portfolio Pricing – A carrier's maximum discount, designed to capture business.

Pre-Bid and Submittal Meeting – A meeting set up to help bidders understand the requirements of a solicitation.

Prequalification – Screening used to consider a potential vendor's financial capability, performance history, and management.

Proposal – Document submitted in response to a solicitation to perform work or services at a specified price, time frame, and under prescribed terms and conditions.

Proposer – Person or entity who submits a proposal in response to a solicitation.

Purchasing and Procurement – The act and responsibility for acquiring goods and services.

Rejected Bidder – A bidder rejected for one or more reasons.

Request for Information – General invitation to persons or firms who possess knowledge of the scope of required goods or services.

Request for Proposals (RFP) – Solicitation document requesting submittal of a proposal in response to the parameters and scope of required goods or services.

Request for Qualifications (RFQ) – Solicitation document requesting persons or entities submit qualifications or specialized expertise in response to the parameters and scope of required goods or services.

Responsive – Bidder or proposer has prepared and submitted all required documents under the solicitation.

Responsible – Bidder or proposer has demonstrated an ability to perform and deliver under the terms of the solicitation.

Revenue Tier – A specific revenue tier or band, based on the weekly revenue generated from a carrier's customer. The tier will often determine the customer discount.

Rolling Average – Carriers use rolling averages to determine the average weekly revenue level a customer provides them.

Sealed Bid – Bid submitted in a sealed envelope or package to prevent dissemination of its contents before the deadline for submitting bids.

Sole Source – A vendor that is exclusively or uniquely qualified to provide goods or services.

Strategic Sourcing – A concept of purchasing where the objective is to purchase goods or services that will reduce costs, increase managerial effectiveness, and improve efficiency.

Subcontractor – A person or entity that has an agreement with a contractor to perform a portion of a contract.

Terms and Conditions – Legal terms and conditions contained in solicitations and contracts.

Vendor – Entity or individual that provides or expresses interest in providing goods and services.

Source: Roadway, "Glossary – Industry and Roadway Terms," http://www.roadway.com, accessed July 2006; FedEx, "Glossary," http://www.fedex.com/ca_english/shippingguide/glossary.html?link=2, accessed December 2004; UPS, "Glossary," http://www.ups.com/content/us/en/resources/glossary/index.html, accessed December 2004; Michael Erickson, "Small Parcel Service," http://ww.dcvelocity.com/articles/feb2004/ enroute.cfm, accessed June 2006.

APPENDIX 10: Contracting Cycle

Successful shipper-carrier contracts rely on careful and detailed preparation. Both parties need a clear understanding of contract requirements. A contract can be a brief document of one or two pages or one that consists of hundreds of pages. The following diagram illustrates key phases of a typical transportation contract cycle.

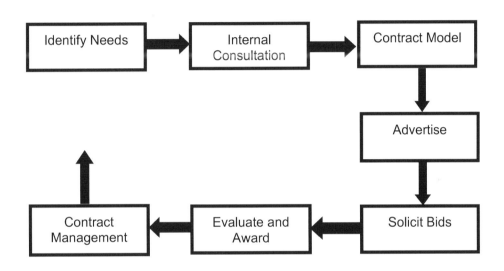

Identify Needs

Clearly identify current and future needs before selecting a carrier and acquiring services.

Internal Consultation

After identifying needs, it is important for management to consult with all internal departments the contract will affect.

Contract Model

Shippers must evaluate and select the appropriate contract model. There are many contract models, two of which are competitive bidding and negotiation.

Advertise

The objective is to identify and prequalify carriers. Shippers will invite carriers to submit an expression of interest for a particular contract. Shippers will assess each carrier's ability to meet their needs before issuing a bid package.

Solicit Bids

Shippers invite carriers who fit their firms' bid requirements to submit a bid package.

Evaluate and Award

Shippers evaluate bids against predetermined requirements specified in the bid package and notify the successful bidder. Within limits of confidentiality, shippers will endeavor to offer unsuccessful bidders feedback related to their bid.

Contract Management

Shippers are responsible for monitoring and managing contract performance to insure compliance.

Source: John E. Tyworth, Joseph L. Cavinato and C. John Langley, Jr., *Traffic Management*, (Prospect Heights, IL: Westland Press, Inc., 1991), 194-211. Also, Corporation of London. "The procurement process." http://www.cityoflondon.gov.uk/Corporation/about_us/purchasing_andcontracts/what_the_corporation_buys/procurement_process.

SECTION V — GLOSSARY – SHIPPING TERMS

SECTION V

GLOSSARY SHIPPING TERMS

FOLLOWING ARE DOMESTIC AND international shipping terms commonly used in the parcel delivery environment and freight transportation industry:

49 CFR: Title 49 of the Code of Federal Regulations (CFR) contains Hazardous Materials Regulations (HMR) that govern shipping hazardous material.

A

Accessorial (also called Surcharges and Assessorial Charges) are charges carriers apply for performing services beyond normal pickup and delivery, such as inside delivery, address correction, notification, and storage charges.

Acknowledgment of Delivery is a service where consignee signs a confirmation receipt and returns it to the shipper.

Actual Class is the classification assigned to an article or commodity as published in NMF 100 series.

Airfreight Forwarder provides pickup and delivery services under its own tariff, consolidates shipments into larger units, prepares shipping documentation, and tenders shipments to the airlines. Normally, airfreight forwarders, referred to as "indirect air carriers," do not operate their own aircraft.

Air Shipping Document (ASD) is a three-part form used to ship packages by air. It contains the shipper's address label, tracking label, and shipping record.

Air Waybill is a forwarding (or carrying) agreement between shipper and air carrier, used as a receipt for cargo and as a contract of carriage.

Audit, in reference to freight bills, is the term used to determine their accuracy.

Auditing involves checking the freight bill for errors, such as correct rate and weight to determine the correct transportation charge.

Automated Export System (AES) is the United States Census Bureau's Internet-based system for filing Shipper's Export Declaration (SED) information to Customs and Border Protection.

Automated Export System (AES) Transaction Number identifies an export shipment. Generated by AESDirect, the number combines the Exporter Identification Number (EIN) and the Export and Reference Number (ERN).

B

Backhaul is the return trip of a transportation asset.

Bar Code is a series of alternating bars and spaces printed or stamped on products, labels, or other media, representing encoded information and read by electronic readers.

Bill of Lading is a legal contract that services three main functions: (1) a receipt for goods delivered to the carrier for shipment, (2) a description of the goods, and (3) evidence of title to the relative goods, if "negotiable."

Bonded Carriers are licensed by U.S. Customs and carry customs-controlled merchandise between customs points.

Bond In is when goods are held or transported under customs control until import duties or other charges are paid.

Booking is the act of requesting cargo space and equipment aboard a vessel.

Bracing is a method of securing items inside a carrier's vehicle to prevent damage.

Break Bulk is the process of separating a shipment (at a breakbulk terminal) into individual shipments for routing to different destinations.

Broker is an independent contractor paid by a carrier or shipper to arrange motor carrier transportation.

Bundling is when two or more products are combined into one transaction, to obtain a single price.

C

Cabotage is a Federal law that requires the use of U.S. built and registered ships for coastal and intercoastal traffic.

Cargo is merchandise carried by a transportation carrier.

Carmack is a transportation industry term that refers to loss or damage of cargo.

Carrier is an enterprise engaged in the business of transporting goods.

Cartage Agent is a carrier who performs pickup or delivery service for other carriers.

Cell-by-cell Pricing is a pricing formula used to determine a rate applicable to a specific weight and zone combination.

Certificate of Insurance is a negotiable document that indicates insurance is secured under an open policy to cover loss or damage to a shipment while in transit.

Certificate of Origin is a certified document presented to customs authorities that show the national origin of goods for import.

Certificate of Public Convenience and Necessity is the granting of operating authority to a common carrier. Certificate specifies the commodities carrier may haul and the routes it may use.

Certificated Carrier is a for-hire air carrier that is subject to economic regulation.

Chargeable Weight is the shipment weight used to determine freight charges.

Claim:
Cargo Claim is a demand made upon a transportation carrier for payment because of freight loss or damage alleged to have occurred while the shipment was in its possession.

Overcharge Claim is a demand made upon a transportation carrier for the refund of an overcharge.

Class I Carrier is a classification of regulated carriers based on annual operating revenues—motor carriers of property, $5 million; railroads, $50 million; motor carriers of passengers, $3 million.

Class II Carrier is a classification of regulated carriers based on annual operating revenues— motor carriers of property, $1-5 million; railroads, $10-50 million; motor carriers of passengers, $3 million.

Class III Carriers is a classification of regulated carriers based on annual operating revenues—motor carriers of property, $1 million; railroads, $10 million.

Class Rates is to group goods or commodities under one general heading. All the commodities in the group make up a class and receive "class rates."

Classification is an alphabetical listing of commodities and the applicable class or rating.

Collect on Delivery (COD) is a shipment for which the carrier is responsible for collecting the sale price of the goods shipped to the consignee, before delivery.

Commodities are any articles of commerce; goods transported.

Commodity Rate is transportation rate for a specific commodity from its origin to its destination.

Concealed Loss is a shortage or damaged shipment not evident at delivery.

Consignee is a person or place that receives a shipment.

Consignment is when goods are shipped to an overseas agent before purchase, under an agreement the consignee will sell the goods.

Consignor is the shipper of goods or a transportation movement.

Consolidation is the process of collecting smaller shipments to form a larger shipment.

Container is anything in which goods are packed; used for the transport of goods.

Containerization is the technique of placing a quantity of items in a box-shaped container for storage, protection, and transport, as one unit.

Cost and Freight is a billing option for international shipments where the shipper pays the transportation charges to the port of import and the consignee (or recipient) pays remaining charges.

Courier Service is a door-to-door service for goods and documents.

Cross Docking is to move goods directly from the receiving dock to the shipping dock.

Cube-out is the term used when a piece of equipment has reached its volumetric capacity before reaching the carrier's allowable weight limit.

Cubic Capacity is the carrying capacity of a transport vehicle, according to its measurement in cubic feet.

Customhouse Broker is an individual or firm licensed to enter and clear goods through customs.

Customs is the authority assigned to collect duties, taxes, or other charges levied by a country on imports and exports.

D

Dangerous Goods are commodities that, when transported, pose some form of danger to people, animals, the environment, or a carrier.

Declared Value is the value a shipper places on a shipment when requesting additional insurance coverage against loss or damage.

Delivered Duty Paid is a situation where the shipper pays both shipping charge and duty taxes on an international shipment.

Delivery Codes designate delivery destinations as either rural or urban.

Delivery Density is the number of packages delivered at one time to one place. The higher the delivery density, the lower the carrier's per-package costs.

Delivery Information Acquisition Devices (DIAD) enable carriers to record delivery information electronically at the point of delivery and upload the data to the carrier's computer mainframe.

Delivery Receipt is a document dated and signed by consignee or its agent during delivery of a shipment.

Density is the physical characteristic that measures a commodity's mass per unit volume or pounds per cubic foot.

Density Rate is a rate based upon the commodity's density and shipment weight.

Detention is a penalty for exceeding free time allowed for loading and unloading under the terms of the agreement with the carrier.

Dimensional Weight is a calculation of a shipment's weight based on the IATA volumetric standard instead of its actual weight.

Dispatch is the act of sending a driver on a specific route with the required shipping papers.

Diversion is the process of changing a shipment's destination while the shipment is en route.

Dock is a platform, the same height as the trailer floor, where trucks are loaded and unloaded.

Duty-ad Valorem is a tax imposed on imported merchandise based on its value.

Duty Compound is a tax imposed on imported merchandise, based on value as well as the net weight or number of pieces.

Duty Drawbacks is an import and export incentive where a customs agency refunds a portion of the duty tax.

Duty-Free refers to classes of goods that are able to enter a country free of duty or not subject to taxes.

Duty Specific is a tax imposed on imported merchandise based on the net weight or number of pieces only.

E

Electronic Data Interchange (EDI) is the electronic transmission of business documents.

E-mail Ship Notification is a service that allows shippers to notify multiple parties by e-mail regarding details of a shipment, including tracking information.

Embargo is a prohibition upon exports or imports.

End User is the final buyer of a product or service.

En route is the term used for goods in transit or on the way to a destination.

Exempt Carrier is a for-hire carrier that is exempt from economic regulations.

Exempt Commodity is a commodity, such as agricultural and forestry products, that is exempt from federal regulation.

Expediting is an attempt to speed up a shipment's delivery.

Export is the physical movement of goods out of a country.

Export Broker is an enterprise that brings together buyers and sellers for a fee, and then eventually withdraws from the transaction.

Export Declaration is a formal statement that declares full details of an export commodity at a port of exit.

Export License is a license issued by the shipper's export country, which permits the licensee to export designated goods to specified destinations.

Extended Area Surcharge is a charge applied for delivery to, or collection from, an area that falls outside the carrier's service area.

F

Flexible Parcel Insurance is coverage for items ineligible for standard carrier liability programs, such as event tickets and negotiable instruments. It also allows the shipper to insure items for a value greater than their actual value.

Forwarding Agent is a person authorized by a principal party to perform the services required to facilitate the export of items from the U.S.

Free along Side (FAS) means the buyer is responsible for loading the goods onto the transport vessel and paying all the cost of shipping beyond that location.

Free on Board (FOB) Destination changes the location where title and risk pass. Under this arrangement, title and risk remain with the seller until he/she has delivered the freight to the delivery location specified in the contract.

Free on Board (FOB) Origin means the title and risk pass to the buyer when the seller makes delivery to the carrier. The parties may agree to have title and risk pass at a different time or to allocate freight charges by a written agreement.

Free Time is the period allowed for the removal or accumulation of cargo before charges become applicable.

Free Trade Agreement is an arrangement that establishes unimpeded exchange and flow of goods and services between trading partners, regardless of national barriers.

Freight is any article or commodity shipped.

Freight-all-kinds (FAK) is rate-making process where a carrier applies a single class to all of a shipper's articles or commodities.

Freight Bill is a shipping document prepared by the carrier describing the freight, its weight, and freight charges.

Freight Broker is any person who sells transportation without physically providing it.

Freight Charge is the rate collected for transporting freight.

Freight Quotation is a quotation from a carrier or freight forwarder covering the cost of transport between two specified locations.

G

General Tariff applies to countries that do not enjoy either preferential or most-favored-nation tariff treatment.

Goods is a term associated with more than one definition: (1) common term indicates movable property, merchandise, or wares; (2) materials which are used to satisfy demands; (3) whole or part of cargo received from the shipper, including any equipment supplied by the shipper.

Gross Weight is the total weight of the vehicle and the payload of freight or passengers.

H

Harmonized System is a system developed by the Customs Cooperation Council (now known as the World Customs Organization) for classifying goods in international trade.

Hazardous Material is material or substance designated as hazardous by the U.S. Department of Transportation if its transport poses an unreasonable risk to health and safety or property.

Hub is a central location for inbound traffic from many cities and from which outbound traffic is fed to other areas.

Hundredweight (CWT) is the abbreviated equivalent of one hundred pounds.

I

Igloos are pallets and containers used in air transportation.

Import is the physical movement of goods into a country.

Import Restrictions refer to controls a country imposes to control the volume and types of goods from other countries.

In Bond refers to a shipment moving under bond from a United States point of entry to an interior destination or a border location for clearance.

Incentive Rate is a rate intended to induce a shipper to ship heavier volumes.

Inland Bill of Lading is a carriage contract used in transport from a shipping point overland to the exporter's international carrier location.

Insured Value is the amount in U.S. dollars for which a package is protected against loss or damage.

Integrated Carrier is an airfreight company that offers a blend of transportation services, such as air carriage, freight forwarding, and ground handling.

Interchange is the transfer of cargo and equipment from one carrier to another carrier, in a joint freight transportation move.

Interline is when two or more motor carriers work together to transport a shipment to its final destination.

Intermediate Destination is a stopping point for a shipment before the final destination.

International Air Transport Association (IATA) is an international rate bureau for air carriers' passenger and freight movements.

In-Transit Bond is a bond that allows cargo to be transported or warehoused under U.S. Customs and Border Protection supervision.

International Safe Transit Association (ISTA) is an organization that develops packaging methods and logistics systems to prevent or reduce damage to a shipment.

Interstate Commerce is to transport persons or property between states.

Intrastate Commerce is to transport persons or property between points within a state.

Issuing Carrier is the carrier shown on the bill of lading and with whom the contract of carriage exists.

J

Joint Rate is the rate charged when two or more carriers combine services to transport a shipment.

L

Lading refers to the cargo in a transportation vehicle.

Less-Than-Truckload refers to shipments of goods or merchandise that comprise less than a truckload in volume, typically less than 10,000 pounds.

Line-haul is to move freight between cities or between a carrier's origin and destination terminals.

Load Optimization is the practice of maximizing the use of transportation assets, such as vehicle space, to maximize revenue and minimize operating costs.

Lumping is to assist a carrier's driver load and unload a vehicle.

M

Manifest is a list of cargo that pertains to a specific shipment, grouping of shipments, or a piece of equipment.

Marks of Origin are physical markings on a product that indicate the country of origin.

Matrix Pricing is pricing discounts determined by weight or zone for each service.

Mileage Rate is a rate based on the number of miles a commodity ships.

Minimum Charge is the carrier's lowest charge for handling a shipment.

Minimum Weight is the weight carrier tariffs specify as being the minimum shipment weight required to use its various rate structures.

Motor Carrier is an enterprise that offers transportation service.

Multimodal (also called Intermodal) refers to the practice of using more than one mode of transportation (rail, ocean, air, and ground) to deliver a shipment.

Multiple Package Shipment is a shipment that consists of individual packages, listed on the same shipping document, consigned to the same consignee address.

Multiple Parcel Stop is a delivery stop where the consignee regularly receives many packages.

N

National Motor Freight Classification (NMFC) is a tariff published by motor carriers containing rules and commodity descriptions; used to classify freight for rating a freight bill.

Net Minimums are the minimum rates set by the carrier, which ensure the carrier minimum revenue for delivering the shipment.

North American Free Trade Agreement (NAFTA) is a free trade agreement that comprises Canada, the U.S., and Mexico.

O

Order Notify (also called Negotiable Bill of Lading) requires the consignee to surrender the original endorsed bill of lading upon delivery of a shipment.

Origin Location is the location where a shipment originates; used to determine transportation cost.

Overage is when the number of units shipped is greater than the quantity shown on shipping documents.

P

Packing List is a document that gives a detailed description and quantity of items shipped.

Pallet is a platform device used for moving and storing goods.

Piggyback is a trailer that is loaded onto a rail flatcar for transport.

Port of Entry is where foreign goods are inspected and cleared for entry into a country.

PRO is an acronym for the "progressive rotating order" number assigned to a shipment and serves as a carrier's tracking and invoice number.

Proportional Rate is a rate lower than the regular rate for a shipment that has prior or subsequent moves.

R

Ramp-up Period is the grace period for target discounts before a contract goes into effect.

Rates are the established charges for the transport of goods.

Reconsignment is a carrier service that permits a shipper to change a shipment's destination or consignee.

Redirect Package is a delivery option for when a package cannot be delivered at the specified address.

Released-value Rates is where the carrier's maximum liability for damage is less than the full value, and in return, the carrier offers a lower rate.

Restricted and Prohibited Articles are commodities a carrier will not transport.

Revenue Tier is a specific revenue tier or band carriers provide, which depends on the weekly average revenue received from a shipper.

Reverse Logistics is the return of a shipment or order from the consignee back to the shipper.

Rolling Average is used by carriers to determine the average weekly revenue levels a shipper provides them.

Route is the complete movement of a shipment from its origin to its destination.

S

Ship Date is the date a consignee tenders a shipment to a carrier

Ship from Location is the location where a shipment originates.

Shipment is a user-defined unit containing goods (single or multiple units) and requires transportation from one location to another.

Shipping Documents are papers, such as bill of lading, packing list, and delivery receipt, which accompany a shipment as it moves through a carrier's delivery system.

Shortage occurs when the number of units received is less than quantity shown on shipping documents.

Single Entry Bond (SEB) is a one-time bond issued to ensure compliance with U.S. laws and regulations.

Stench Packaging is a packaging system designed to protect against the release of odors in case of leakage from a primary receptacle.

Stretch-wrap is a thin, elastic, plastic material shippers wrap around items on a pallet for containment.

T

Tare Weight is the weight of the vehicle when empty.

Tariff is a document that contains carrier rules and other provisions, which govern transport.

Tariff Schedule is a comprehensive list of goods that a country imports and the applicable import duties.

Tender is a request for space and equipment with a motor carrier.

Terminal is a location or facility used for handling and temporary storage of shipments, as they are loaded and unloaded or transferred between enterprises.

Terms and Conditions is the part of a carrier's shipping contract that contains the general terms and conditions under which the carrier is engaged to transport commodities.

Third-party Logistics is an outsource strategy where a company involves the use of another company to manage its assets.

Time-in-transit is the number of days a shipment is in transit from pickup to delivery.

Through Bill of Lading is a bill of lading that covers both the domestic (inland) and international carriage of an export shipment.

Ton-mile is a transportation output measure that reflects the shipment's weight and the distance it travels.

Tracing is determining a shipment's location during a move.

Tracking is a carrier's system of recording the movement intervals of a shipment from origin to destination.

Traffic Management is the buying, controlling, and management of transportation services for a shipper or consignee, or both.

Trailer on Flat Car (TOFC) is the carriage of intermodal containers, on a rail flat car, while the container is attached to the chassis.

Tramp is an international water carrier that has no fixed route or published schedule. A shipper charters a tramp ship for a particular voyage or a given time period.

Transit Time is the time that elapse time between a shipment's pickup and its delivery.

Truckload (TL) is a large-volume shipment from a single customer that typically weighs over 10,000 pounds or occupies trailer space so no other shipment can be loaded.

U

UN Number is an internationally accepted four-digit number used to identify hazardous material.

Unit Train is the entire rail train movement between an origin and destination.

Unitize is the process of consolidating items into one unit.

U.S. Shipper's Export Declaration is a standard United States government form required for all U.S. exports with commodities, valued at US$2,500 or higher

V

Valuation Charge is a carrier's charge to shippers who declare the value of its shipment exceeds the carriers' limits of liability.

Vender is a firm or individual that supplies goods or services; the seller.

W

Waybill is a nonnegotiable document prepared by or for the carrier at the point of shipment origin. The document shows point of origin, destination, route, consignor, consignee, description of shipment, and the amount charged for the transport service.

Z

Zone is a service area which carriers use to base their shipping rate.

NOTE: *The above Glossary is a modification of shipping terms compiled from various sources. It is limited and not presented as a definitive source of information.*

SECTION VI — NOTES

SECTION I

NOTES

1. For a definition of the parcel delivery industry, see Edward K. Morlok, Bradley F. Nitzberg, Karthik Balasubramaniam, and Mark L. Sand, "The Parcel Service Industry in the U.S.: Its Size and Role in Commerce," accessed August 1, 2000, http://www.seas.upenn.edu/sys/logistics/ parcelstudy.html.
2. Alan Robinson, "Competition Within the United States Parcel Delivery Market," accessed July 15, 2005, http://www.postcom.org/public/articles/2003articles/panel_competition.htm; also U.S. Treasury, "A Brief History of the Package Delivery Industry," accessed April 13, 2005, http://wwwtreas.gov/offices/domestic-finance/usps/docs/panel_history_final1.doc.
3. Morlok, "The Parcel Service Industry in the U.S.: Its Size and Role in Commerce," 33-35.
4. Mark Hendricks, "Mass Appeal: Find Out How Mass Customization – One of the Hottest Trends in Business – Can Work for You," accessed May 26, 2009, http://findarticles.com/p/articles/mi_m)DTI/os_n8_v24ai_18517692/; also Joseph Pine II, Wikipedia, "Mass Customization," accessed May 19, 2009, http://en.wikipedia.org/wiki/Mass_customization.
5. FedEx Global Newsroom, "FedEx Refreshes Web Tracking Tools," accessed May 21, 2009, http://news.vanfedex.com/node/12636/print.
6. Wikipedia, "Core Competency," accessed May 20, 2009, http://en.wikipedia.org/wiki/Core_competency.
7. Bureau of Transportation Statistics, "Commodity Flow Survey" (2007), Table 1a, accessed May 3, 2010, http://www.bis.gov/publications/commodity_flow_survey/final_tables_december_2009/html.
8. Morlok, "The Parcel Service Industry in the U.S.: Its Size and Role in Commerce," 36-37.
9. Section adapted from Alan Robinson, "Competition within the United States Parcel Delivery Market."
10. Dr. Jean-Paul Rodrigue, "UPS: Logistical Management of Distribution Networks," Hofstra University, accessed April 23, 2008, http://people.hofstra.edu/geotrans /eng/ch5en/appl5en/ch5a2en.html
11. Wikipedia, "United Parcel Service," accessed May 21, 2010, http://en.wikipedia.org/wiki/United_Parcel_Service
12. Wikipedia, "United Parcel Service."
13. Answers.com, "FedEx History," accessed July 16, 2006, http://www.answers.com/topic/fedex-1.

14. Wikinvest, "FedEx Corporation," accessed June 2, 2009, http://www.wikinvest.com/stock/FedEx_(FDX).
15. Wikipedia, "FedEx Corporation," accessed May 21, 2010, http://www.wikipedia.org/wiki/FedEx.
16. Section was adapted from Answers.com, "United States Postal Service," accessed August 17, 2006, http://www.answers.com/topic/united-states-postal-service.
17. USPS, "Postal Service Ends 2009 with $3.8 Billion Loss," accessed May 21, 2010, http://www.usps.com/communications/newsroom/2009/pr09_098.htm.
18. YRC Tariff 100, Item 753, "Residential Pickup & Delivery Service," accessed June 21, 2009, http://my.yrc.com.
19. IoPP Transport Packaging Committee, "Guide to Packaging for Small Parcel Shipments," (3/1/02, revised 3/17/03, 12/14/04, 7/25/05).
20. USPS Domestic Mail Manual (DMM), Issue 58, "General Mailability Standards," accessed June 2009, http://pe.usps.com/archive.asf.
21. Section adapted from IoPP's, "Guide to Packaging for Small Parcel Shipments."
22. Section was developed from Alan Robinson, "Competition within the United States Parcel Delivery Market."
23. Jason H. Smith, "Shape-based Pricing – Not Your Standard Postage Increase," accessed June 18, 2009, http://www.buyerzone.com/mailroom/postage_meters/shape-based-pricing.html.
24. Tiffany Wiazlowski, "Parcel Carriers Encroach on Changing LTL Sector," accessed June 30, 2009, http://www.allbusiness.com/transportation/road-transportation-trucking-trucking/11435529.
25. Dan Goodwill, "The Price of Leadership in LTL," accessed October 8, 2008, http://www.ctl.ca/issues/story.aspx?aid=1000215361&type=Print%20Archives.
26. William B. Cassidy, "Parcel Carriers Claim Bigger Share of Trucking," accessed May 23, 2010, http://www.joc.com/trucking/.
27. Wiazlowski (quoting Satish Jindel), "Parcel Carriers Encroach on Changing LTL."
28. Tom Krueger, "Wisely Select Your Carrier to Reduce Parcel Delivery Costs," accessed June 29, 2009, http://www.targetmarketingmag.com/.
29. Toby B. Gooley, "Why Shippers Like Zoneskipping," accessed July 8, 2009, http://blog.fmidm.com/?p=710.
30. Paul Miller, "FedEx Will Purchase Consolidator Parcel Direct," accessed July 8, 2009, http://www.printthis.clickability.com/.
31. Gooley, "Why Shippers Like Zoneskipping".
32. The Distribution Management Group, Inc., "Postal Colsolidators – Here Today, Acquired Tomorrow," accessed July 7, 2009, http://www.dmgincorporated.com/article_200410.html.
33. Bill Kuipers, "Postal Power," accessed July 8, 2009, http://www.printthisclickability.com.
34. Dave Ross, "The History of E-commerce," accessed July 9, 2009, http://communication.howstuffworks.com/history-e-commerce.htm.

35 Wikipedia, "Electronic Commerce," accessed July 13, 2009, http://en.wikipedia.org/wiki/Electronic_commerce.
36 A. Srikanth, "E-commerce: A B2B Guide," accessed September 4, 2006, http://www.hinduonnet.com/businessline/iw/2000/05/28/stories/0728g101.htm.
37 Ken Walsh, "Business-to-consumer E-commerce," accessed July 7, 2006, http://projects.bus.lsu.edu/independent_study/vdhing1/b2c/.
38 Ecommerce-Land, "History of Ecommerce," accessed July 14, 2009, http://www.ecommerce-land.com/history_ecommerce.html.
39 The Knowledge Exchange, "An Introduction into E-commerce," accessed July 18, 2009, http://www.marcbowles.com/ sample_courses/amc/ec1/ec1_3.htm.
40 Linda Rosencrance, "E-commerce Sales to Boom for Next 5 Years," accessed July 20, 2009, http://www.computerworld.com/s/article/9061108/.
41 Erick Schonfeld, "Forrester Forecast: Online Retail Sales Will Grow to $250 Billion by 2014," accessed May 27, 2010, http://techcrunch.com/2010/03/08.
42 U.S. Census, "E-Stats (2010)," accessed June 10, 2010, http://www.census.gov/estats.
43 Section was developed from University of California, Irvine document titled, "Issues in Emerging Home Delivery Operations," accessed September 7, 2006, http://www.uctc.net/scripts/countdown.pl?716.pdf.
44 Satish Jindel, "Delivering E-Commerce," accessed September 2006, http://www.jindel.com/Aircargoworld0399print.htm.
45 Satish Jindel, "Transforming the Parcel Industry at the Speed of Business," accessed May 11, 2003, http://www.shipmatrix.com/PressRoom.
46 FedEx Ground ,"Our Growth Starts at the Top," accessed July 16, 2006, http://company.monster.com/rpscen/.
47 Rethink Research Associates, "Competition Takes FedEx and UPS to the Forefront of the Technological Innovation," accessed October 28 2006, http://www.findarticles.com/p/articles/mi_m0PAT/is_2004_July/ai_n6148566/print.
48 Wikipedia, "Barcode," accessed July 23, 2009, http://en.wikipedia.org/wiki/Barcode.
49 Links999 , "Introduction to Barcode," accessed June 9, 2004, http://www.links999.net/hardware/barcode/barcode_introduction.html.
50 Zebra Technologies Corporation white paper, "Improving Parcel & Postal Operations with Bar Code Printing," accessed May 30, 2008, http://www.zebra.com.
51 Dataintro Software , "Two-Dimensional Bar Code Overview," accessed April 5, 2009, http://www.dataintro.com/Lit/wp2dbarcodes.pdf.
52 Wikipedia, "Radio-frequency Identification," accessed November 1, 2009, http://en.wikipedia.org/wiki/Radio-frequency_identification; "Active Tag (Active RFID Tag)," accessed November 8, 2009, http://www.technology.com/ct/Technology-Article.asp?ArtNum=21; and "Passive RFID Tag (or Passive Tag)," accessed November 8, 2009, http://www.technology.com/ct/Technology-Article.asp?ArtNum=47.
53 Ed McKenna, "It's 2 A.M. Want to Know Where Your Shipment Is," accessed October 28, 2006, http://www.glscs.com/archives/10.98.shipment.htm ?adcode=75.

54. Printek, Inc., white paper, "Five Tips for Selecting the Best Mobile Printer," accessed November 8, 2009, http://www.printek.com/pdf/whitepaper.
55. Galen Gruman, "UPS vs FedEx: Head-to-Head on Wireless," accessed August 24, 2006, http://www.cio.com/archive/060104/ups.html.
56. Rethink Research Associates, "Competition Takes FedEx and UPS to the Forefront of the Technological Innovation."
57. UPS Pressroom , "Package Flow Technologies: Innovation at Work," accessed October 5, 2005, http://www.pressroom.ups.com/mediakits/factsheet/0,2305,1134,00.html.
58. UPS Pressroom, "The UPS Delivery Information Acquisition Device (DIAD IV)," accessed April 25, 2008, http://www.pressroom.ups.com/mediakits/popups/factsheet/0,1889,1077,00.html.
59. Arik Hesseldahl, "FedEx Has a New Gadget," accessed July 27, 2009, http://www.forbes.com/2002/11/26/cx_ah_1126fdx.html.
60. Gruman, "UPS vs FedEx: Head-to-Head on Wireless."
61. Diamond Phoenix Corporation, "Sortation Systems," accessed July 24, 2009, http://www.diamondphoenix.com/page.php?page=sortation-system.
62. James A Cooke, "Diversionary Tactics," accessed July 24, 2009, http://www.dcvelocity.com/print/?article_id=906.
63. China Daily, "FedEx Unpackaging on Globalization," accessed August 2009, http://www.chinadaily.com.cn/en/doc/2003-10/23/content_274803.htm.
64. Oxford Economic Forecasting, "The Impact of the Express Delivery Industry on the Global Economy," accessed October 4, 2008, http://www.global-express.org/doc/Global_Express_Impact_Study.pdf
65. Mark A. Taylor, Taylor Systems Engineering Corporation white paper "Globalization Means Small Parcel Shippers Need to Get Ready for Shipping Internationally," accessed October 8, 2009, http://www.TaylorSystyems Engineering.com.
66. Robert Dahl, "ACMG Releases Its Sixteenth Annual U.S. Domestic Air Freight and Express Industry Performance Analysis," accessed October 1, 2010, http://www.cargogacts.com.
67. Robert Malone, "Airfreight Grows Globally," accessed October 10, 2008, http://www/forbes.com/2006/03/15/airfreight-forwarding-shipping-cx_rm_0316airfreight.html.
68. Wikinvest, "FedEx," accessed June 1, 2009, http://www.wikinvest.com/stock/FedEx_FDX.
69. Wikipedia, "United Parcel Service," accessed April 8, 2011, http://en.wikipedia.org/wiki/United_Parcel_Service.
70. Peter Bradley, "The World in One Neat Package," accessed August 30, 2009, http://www.dcvelocity.com/print/?article_id=1731 and Andrew K. Burger, "Special Delivery: Bringing SMBs into the Global Shipping Network," accessed August 31, 2009, http://www.crmbuyer.com/story/61034.html.

SECTION II

NOTES

71 IoPP Transport Packaging Committee, "Guide to Packaging for Small Parcel Shipments," [3/1/02, revised 3/17/03, 12/14/04, 7/25/05].

72 USPS, "General Mailability Standards," *Domestic Mail Manual (DMM)* 58, accessed December 9, 2004, http://pe.usps.com/archive.asf.

73 For example, USPS publishes requirements and guidelines in module C of the Domestic Mail Manual (DMM), International Mail Manual (IMM), and Publication 2 (2002).

74 USPS, "Package Adequacy," *Publication 2*, Section 1 (2002), accessed July 5, 2010, http://pe.usps.com/text/pub2/pub2c1_006.html.

75 UPS, "Original Manufacturer's Packaging," accessed January 16, 2010, http://www.ups.com/content/us/en/resources/ship/packaging/materials/original.html also Marking Solution Ltd., "Parcel Packaging Advice," accessed January 16, 2010, http://www.appletattoo.com/packaging.html.

76 Conpac Group, "Custom Packaging Solutions," accessed April 27, 2003, http://www.conpacgroup.com/new_page_11.htm.

77 UPS, "Internal Packaging," accessed January 16, 2010, http://www.ups.com/content/us/en/resources/ship/packaging/materials/insulation.html also Wapedia, "Cushioning," accessed January 14, 2010, http://wapedia.mobi/en/Cushioning.

78 This section was developed from USPS, "Closing, Sealing, and Reinforcing," Publication 2, Section 4 (2002), and other references, as indicated.

79 Wikipedia, "Adhesive," accessed July 28, 2010, http://en,Wikipedia.org/wiki/Adhesive.

80 Thistothat.com, "How We Select Glue," accessed January 16, 2010, http://www.thistothat.com/glue/ general.shtml also AZoM, "Adhesives – An Introduction," accessed July 31, 2010, http://www.azom.com/details.asp?ArticleID=189.

81 Signode, "Strapping," accessed August 8, 2010, http://www.signode.com/na/protective_packaging/strapping.htm.

82 Imperial Paper Company, "Method of Box Closure," accessed January 16, 2010, http://www.imperialpaper.com/box_closure.html also Great Little Box Company, "Box Closure Methods," accessed January 16, 2010, http://www.greatlittlebox.com/packaging/boxclosures/.

83 Wikipedia, "Pressure Sensitive Tape," accessed August 1, 2010, http://en.wikipedia.org/wiki/Pressure_sensitive_tape.

84 For details related to standards methods of box closure, refer to ASTM International, ASTM Standard D 1974, "Practice for Methods of Closing, Sealing, and Reinforcing Fiberboard Boxes,"
85 UPS, "How to Prepare for Shipping," accessed July 30, 2010, http://www.ups.com/contents/us/en/resources/ship/packaging/guidelines/how_to4.html.
86 UPS, "Boxes, Bytes, and Barcodes," accessed July 30, 2010, http://www.100ups.com/history/technology3.html?srch_pos=94&srch_phr=labels.
87 Russ J. Bragg, "Shipment of Perishable Products and Dry Ice Usage," accessed April 10, 2005, http://cpa.utk.edu/pdfiles/cpa81.pdf.
88 All Tech Industries, "Insulation Factors (K,C,U,R)," accessed December 24, 2009, http://www.alltechinsulation.com/Thermal_U_K_C_R_factors.asp.
89 ToolBase Services, "Vacuum Insulation Panel (VIP)," accessed December 25, 2009, http://www.toolbase.org/.
90 Allan Chen, "Lab's Energy Efficiency Research Benefits Shippers of Perishables," accessed December 25, 2009, http://www.lbs.gov/Science_Articles/Archive/airliner-packaging.html.
91 Polar Tech Industries, "Frequency Asked Questions," accessed December 25 2009, http:www.polar-tech.com/faqs.htm.
92 Deborah Catalano Ruriani, "Shipping Temperature-Sensitive Products," accessed August 7, 2010, http://www.inboundlogistics.com/articles/10tips/10tips1003.shtml.
93 Continental Carbonic Products Inc., "Ship Perishables Products with Dry Ice," accessed November 20, 2009, http://www.continental carbonic.com/dryice/shipping.php.
94 University of California, Environmental Health & Safety, "Dry Ice Shipping," accessed May 10, 2009, http://ehs.ucsc.edu/shipping/pubs/dryice.pdf.
95 FedEx, "Packaging Pointers: Perishable Shipments," accessed July 7, 2009, http://fedex.com/us/services/pdf/PKG_Pointers_Perishables.pdf.
96 Transport Packaging Consultant, "Basic Information for Transport Packaging Design," accessed April 13, 2005, http://www.transport-packaging.com/design-guide.htm.
97 USPS, "Hazardous Materials." Publication 2, Section 7 (2002).
98 Nancy Magnussen, "Introduction – Hazardous Materials Transportation Act," accessed January 20, 2010, http://safety.science.tamu.edu/dot.html.
99 DOT hazard classes are in HM Regulations 49 CFR Parts 171-180.
100 General shipper responsibilities are outlined in 49 CFR Part 173.
101 HM Table (Section 172.101) is used to select the Proper Shipping Name and determine the Basic Shipping Description.
102 Magnussen, "Introduction – Hazardous Materials Transportation Act."
103 Wikipedia, "UN number," accessed January 23, 2010, http://enwikipedia.org/wiki/UN_number.
104 49 CFR 172.519(c) requires that hazardous materials placards meet specified size requirements.

105 UPS, "Labeling," accessed January 23, 2010, http://www.ups.com/content/us/n/resources/ship/hazardous/responsible/labeling.html.
106 U.S. Department of Transportation, "Guide for Preparing Shipping Papers," accessed August 14, 2010, http://hazmatonline.phmsa.dot.gov/.
107 Stacy L. Umstead, "Performance-Oriented Packaging," accessed December 24, 2005, http://www.almc.army.mil/alog/issues/MayHun03/MS878.htm.
108 DDL Inc., "UN and DOT Package Certification," accessed December 19, 2005, http://www.testedandproven.com/haz_mat2.html.
109 UPS, "Stench Packaging," accessed January 10, 2010, http://www.ups.com/content/us/en/resources/ship/hazardous/responsibilities/stench.html.
110 An example would be the limited quantity exceptions provided for certain flammable liquids packages in CFR 49 Section 173.150.
111 Section draws heavily from Unzco Compliance Observer, "Exemptions," accessed December 30, 2005, http://www.unzco.com/compobserver/askarchives.html.
112 LPS Industries, "DOT-SP 8249 Exempt Packaging," accessed May 17, 2008, http://www.lpsind.com/DOTExemptPack.htm.
113 An "approval" is issued under an international standard (for example, ICAO Technical instructions for the Safe Transport of Dangerous Goods by Air).
114 Water (or ocean) is the slowest shipping mode, but usually the lowest transport cost.
115 Unzco, "A Basic Guide to Exporting," accessed January 25, 2010, http://www.unzco.com/basicguide/c10.html.
116 Wikipedia, "International Organization for Standardization," accessed January 25, 2010, http://en.wikipedia.org/wiki/ISO_standards.
117 Wikipedia, "International Organization for Standardization."
118 Wikipedia, "Pallet," accessed November 19, 2009, http://enwikipedia.org/wiki/Pallet.
119 BAEF & LAACC, "Shipping the Product-Labeling," accessed March 29, 2003, http://www.tradeport.org/ts/trade_expert/details/ship/label.html.
120 Southern United States Trade Association, "Basics of Exporting – Export Packing, Marking and Containerization," accessed January 21, 2006, http://www.susta.org/export/packingetc.html.
121 Southern United States Trade Association, "Basics of Exporting."
122 Allied Pallet Company Inc., "Pallet Types & Information," accessed January 25, 2010, http://alliedpallet.net/Information.htm.
123 Corrugated Packaging Council, "Corrugated Benefits," accessed April 18, 2003, http://www.corrugated.org/cpsite/basicbenefit.htm.
124 Discount Box & Shipping Company, "Types of Shipping Boxes," accessed June 11, 2008, http://www.discountbox.com/sh_tbx.htm.
125 John C. Clarke and Jorge A. Marcondes, "What Pallet Manufacturers Should Know about Corrugated Boxes!" accessed August 21, 2010, http://www.unitload.vt.edu/technote/980918/980918.htm.
126 Corrugated Box, "Rules and Regulations," accessed January 2, 2010, http://www.cornerstonebox.com/index.php/Static-Pages/Rules-and-Regulations.html.

127 Alfred H. McKinley, "Corrugated Boxes Commodity or Performance Specified?" accessed April 20, 2003, http://www.transport-packaging.com/ectburst.htm.
128 Smurfit-Stone Container Corporation, "Box Manufacturer's Certificates," accessed March 30, 2006, http://www.smurfit-stone.com.
129 Best Containers Online, "What drum is right for You?," accessed January 26, 2005, http://store.yahoo.com/bestcontainers/55gallondrums.html.
130 Youngstown Barrel & Drum Company, "Performance Oriented Packaging Requirements," accessed January 8, 2006, http://www.ybdco.com/performance.htm.
131 Tradespan Cargo Ltd Freight Forwarding and Consolidations, "Tips & Tricks for Shipping," accessed April 21, 2003, http://www.tradespancanada.com/personal/tips.html.
132 Paper Shipping Sack Manufacturers' Association, Inc., "Industry Scope," accessed August 21, 2010, http://www.pssma.com/index.php?id=10.
133 The Packaging Institute, "Mailing & Courier Bags," accessed August 21, 2010, http://www.packagingknowledge.com/mailing_courier_%20bags.asp.
134 Packaging Price.com Inc., "How Do I Package My Product for Shipping," accessed April 19, 2008, http://www.packagingprice.com.
135 Wikipedia, "Electrostatic Discharge," accessed August 23, 2010, http://en.wikipedia.org/wiki/Electrostatic_discharge
136 The ESD Association, "An Overview of ESD Control Procedures and Materials," accessed August 26, 2010, http://www.ce-mag.com/99ARG/ESD%20Assoc179.html.
137 Mini-Circuits, "The Prevention and Control of Electrostatic Discharge (ESD)," accessed August 25, 2010, http;//www.minicircuits.com/pages/pdfs/an4005.pdf.
138 Gene Chase, "The Electrostatic Discharge (ESD) Packaging Dilemma," accessed April 4, 2006, http://www.electrotechsystems.com/articles/14.pdf.
139 Additional in-depth discussion of static control program materials and procedures can be found in publications such as ESD Handbook, published by the ESD Association.
140 ISTA, "What Are the Differences between ISTA Procedures and ASTM Standards?" accessed August 26, 2010, http://www.ista.org/support/index.php.
141 ISTA, "ISTA Test Procedures," accessed August 26, 2010, http://www.ista.org/pages/procedures/ista-procedures.php.
142 Alfred H. McKinlay, "Measuring Package Performance to Avoid Shipping Damage," accessed August 26, 2010, http://www.astm.org/SNEWS/OCTOBER_2004/mckinlay_oct04.html.
143 UPS, "Packaging," accessed January 23, 2010, http://www.ups.com/content/us/en/resources/ship/hazardous/responsible/packaging.html.
144 UPS, "Vendor Packaging Program," accessed August 24, 2010, accessed http://www.ups-psi.com/businessSol/solutions.vendorpkg.asp?nav=2.

SECTION III

NOTES

145 Section was developed from enVista, "Key Components of Parcel Pricing," accessed March 3, 2008, http://www.envistacorp.com/envista.../Key_Components_of_Parcel_Pricing.pdf.
146 UPS, "Domestic and International Shipping Services," assessed July 7, 2006, http://www.ups.com/content/us/en/bussol/offering/global_transport/package/service_options.html.
147 Dennis Berman, "How to Pay the New Overnight Shipping Game," accessed July 20, 2008, http://www.businessweek.com/enterprise/news/ent70708htm, also Satish Jindel, "Parcel Carriers Should Link Zone-based Pricing to Established Service Standards," accessed July 20, 2008, http://www.jindel.com/Trafficworld0296print.htm.
148 May 2007, USPS adopted a dimensional weight concept, calling it Shape Based Postage Pricing.
149 UPS.com, "Dimensional Weight," accessed February 3, 2010, http://www.ups.com/contents/us/en/resources/prepare/dim_weight.html.
150 Bruce Tompkins, "Are Your Parcel Rate Strategies in Line with Current Trends?" accessed August 5, 2008, http://www.tompkinsinc.com/publications/competitive_edge/articles/1107parcelrates.asp.
151 UPS Freight Tariff UPGF 102-D, Effective: February 1, 2010.
152 Dogwood Ceramic Supply, "Current National Fuel Surcharge Rate," accessed June 26, 2010, http://www.dogwoodceramics.com/fuel_surcharge.htm.
153 Section was adapted from iShip Inc., "Shipping Management for the New Economy: An Internet-delivered Solution," (2002), accessed June 27, 2010, https://iship.com.
154 iShip.com was founded in 1997. UPS purchased business from Stamps.com in May 2001 and renamed it iShip, Inc.
155 SECAP, "Opportunity Can Be Found in Small Packages," November 12, 2006, http://www.secapusa.com/parcel_shipping_tips.htm, also UPS: Business Solutions, "Key Features," June 10, 2010, http://www.ups.com/bussol.
156 Wikipedia, "Value-added Reseller," accessed February 3, 2010, http://en.wikipedia.org/wiki/Value-added_reseller.
157 SECAP, "Tools for the Trade: Multi-Carrier Solutions…" accessed May 16, 2006, http://www.secapusa.com/mail_carrier_solution.htm.
158 Joe Sudar, "What Are Your Shipping Alternatives?" accessed July 5, 2010, http://www.parcelindustry.com/ME2/Audiences /dirmod.asp?sid=&nm=&type=Publishing&.

159 Supply Chain Digest, "Logistics News: Time to Start Looking at Regional Parcel Carriers?" accessed July 5, 2010, http://www.scdigest.com/ASSETS/ON_TARGET/10-01-12-4.php?cid=3128.

160 Kelley Westrick, "Customers Await Your Delivery Decision," accessed September 4, 2006, http://www.workz.com/content/view_content.html?section_id =514&content_id=5383.

161 Roanoke Trade Services Inc., "Declared Value Coverage vs. Cargo Insurance," accessed July 3, 2010, http://www.roanoketrade.com/indlns_cargotrans_declaredvalue-vs-cargoins.pdf.

162 Section was developed from, TransportGistics, "Selecting a Freight Bill Management, Shipment Information and Cost Control Portal," accessed October 1, 2004, http://transportgistics.com/freight%20bill%20audit.htm.

163 Leslie Hansen Harps, "Turning Invoices into Intelligence," accessed October 5, 2004, http://www.inboundlogistics.com/articles/features/1102_feature03.shtml.

164 Source Consulting, "Freight Bill Audit & Carrier Audit Services," accessed July 3, 2010, http://www.sourceconsulting.com/shipping_bill_and_service_audit.html.

165 Mindell Trudell, "Negotiating Shippers' Needs for Meaningful Freight Rates," accessed March 4, 2005, http://www.transportgistics.com/shippers_needs.htm.

166 Schneider Logistics Inc., "The Benefits of Outsourcing Freight Payment Processing," accessed September 25, 2004, http://webapps.schneiderlogistics.com/ company_info/…wp_freightpay.pdf.

167 Wikipedia, "Application Service Provider," accessed February 7, 2010, http://en.wikipedia.org/wiki/Application_service_provider.

168 Thomas A. Foster, "Web Solutions for Transportation Management," accessed January 18, 2005, http://www.glscs.com/archives/10.31.00.Managing.htm.

169 TransportGistics, "Transportation and Distribution Management – Automating the Process," accessed December 20, 2004, http://transportgistics.com/tanddauto.htm.

170 Bill Knaninski, "Understanding Upcharges – Know Where Your Money Goes," accessed January 26, 2004, http://www.psdmag.com/editorial2.asp?ID=134.

171 Dogwood Ceramic Supply, "Common UPS Ground Value-Added Services," accessed September 11, 2008, http://www.dogwoodceramics.com /accessorial_fees.htm.

172 iShip, Inc., "Learn More – Weights, Dimensions, and Packaging," accessed April 19, 2008, http://www.iship.com/priceit/info.asp?info=4.

173 UPS, "Dimensional Weight," accessed March 27, 2003, http://www.ups.com/using /services/packaging/dimwt-guide.html.

174 Toby B. Gooley, "Pay Attention to Packaging!" accessed April 19, 2008, http://www.logisticsmgmt.com/index.asp?layout=articlePrint&articleID=CA6343727.

175 For a discussion of shipment consolidation, see John E. Tyworth, Joseph L. Cavinato, and C. John Langley, Jr., *Traffic Management*, (Illinois: Waveland Press, Inc. 1987), Chapter 10.

176 Michael Bentley, "Carrier Consolidation Services: An Insider Guide to UPS Basic & FedEx SmartPost," accessed June 25, 2010, http://www.envistacorp.com/…/Carrier%20Consolidation%20Services%20An%20 Inside%20Guide%20to90, also

Tom Krueger, "Wisely Select Your Carrier to Reduce Parcel Delivery Costs," accessed June 8, 2010, http://www.targetmarketingmag.com /article.

177 Section developed from Roadway Express Inc., "What You Should Know – Cargo Loss and Damage and Overcharge Claims," accessed June 4, 2006, http://www.roadway.com/tools/tools _claims3.html, and TranSolution Inc., "How to File Freight Claims," accessed May 30, 2006, http://www.transolutioninc.com/howtofile.html.
178 NMF Traffic Association, Inc., STB NMF 100, Item 300105, "Filing of Claims."
179 NMF, Item 300115, "Claims Filed For Uncertain Amounts."
180 NMF, Item 300135, "Reporting Concealed Damage."
181 NMF, Item 300120, "Acknowledgment and Disposition of Claims."
182 NMF, Item 300140, "Inspection of Carrier."
183 NMF, Item 300145, "Failure to Inspect."
184 NMF, Item 300150, "Salvage Retention."
185 NMF, Item 300110, "Documents Required in Support of Claims."
186 Lou Cortese, "Reducing the Risk of Damage, Loss and Claims," accessed August 6, 2004, http://www.inboundlogistics.com/articles/carriers/carriers1103.shtml.
187 This section draws heavily from work by Tyworth, *Traffic Management*, Chapter 8.
188 Toby B. Gooley, "8 Ways to Shrink Your Parcel Costs," accessed July 3, 2010, http://www.insourcesmg.com/resources/8-ways-to-shrink-your-parcel-costs.
189 Rayovac and TransportGistics whitepaper, "Contract Carriage Agreements," accessed March 2, 2005, http://www.insourceaudit.com/ whitepaper/Contract_Carriage_Agreements.asp.
190 James Bucki, "Contract Negotiation Strategies," accessed June 8, 2010, http://operationstech.about.com/od/vendorselection/a/VendorSelect-ContractNegotiation.htm.
191 Tim Sailor, "Choosing Carriers-Big Cost Savings for Shippers May Be Just a Request Away," accessed July 3, 2005, http://www.aircargoworld.com/archives/feat2_aug00.htm.
192 Bill Knasinski, "Looking to Save on Parcel Delivery Costs," accessed July 3, 2010, http://www.genco.com/Transportation-Logistics/parcel-delivery-cost-savings.php.
193 ICC Logistics Services, Inc., "Carrier Selection – Getting Down to Basics," accessed March 3, 2008, http://www.icclogistics.com/
194 Rob Martinez, "How to Choose Between Single and Multisource Parcel Carrier Services," accessed July 2, 2010, http://65.55.72.199/att/Get Attachment.aspx?file=04447fe5-afaf-47f5-b9d5-e9a635d171f7,htm.
195 Riaan Pieterse, "The Tendering Process," accessed June 24, 2005, http://www.sensiblesoftware.com/articles/a/TheTendering-Process.html.
196 Wikipedia, "Contract Management," accessed July 3, 2010, http://en.wikipedia.org/wiki/ Contract_management.
197 Office of Federal Procurement Policy, "A Guide to Best Practices for Contract Administration," accessed July 8, 2010, http://www.acquisition.gov/ bestpractices/bestpcont.html.

Index

4
4G-combination, 69

A
Accessorial charges (referred to as surcharges, ancillary charges, adjustments, and value-added service fees), 97
    basic categories, 108
    monitor and control 109
Aggregation, 6, 113
Aggregator, 107
Air Cargo Management Group (ACMG), 40
Alliances, 98
American Society for Testing and Materials (ASTM), 87
Application Service Provider (ASP), 107
Application Programming Interface (API), 107
ASP system, 107
Associated packaging authorization reference, 120
Assurance level (I, II and III), 88
Audit and freight payment process, 103
Audit and Payment Firms
    audit, payment and information reporting, 104
    freight pre-audit, 103
    post-audit, 104
    pre-audit and payment, 104
Auditing, 103
Automated identification systems, 33

B
Bar code (or barcode), 32, 33, 34, 35, Figure 2
Bar code limitations, 33
Best practice approach, 105

BMC basic rules, 82, Fig. 21
Box certified minimum strength, 81
Box Compression Strength (BCT), 80, Table 8
Box dimensions, 79, Fig. 19
Box Manufacturer's Certificates (BMCs), 46, 81, Fig. 20
    circular, 82
    rectangular, 82
Box performance, 80
Break-bulk, 71
Break-bulk facility, 113
Bridging, 19
Bulk shipping, 71
Business-Business (B2B), 20, 26
Business-Consumer (B2C), 20, 26, 30
Business-originating markets, 20
Business-to-residence sector, 30

C
Carmack Amendment
    rail traffic (49 U.S.C. 11706), 118
    truck traffic (49 U.S.C. 14706), 118
Carrier selection factors, 100, 105, 124
Carrier service guides, 102
Carrier price-making process, 121
Carrier tariffs, 114
Carriers drop box, 14
Certificate of compliance, 69
Certificate period, 69
Certificate schedule, 69
Certification, 62, 83
Characteristics of traditional and e-commerce delivery, 30, Table 5

Charged Device Model (CDM), 86
Chemical classifications, 64
Chemical table, 62, 64, 65, 68
Claim, 114, Table 13
Class 9 materials (referred to as ORM-D consumer commodities), 65
Closure methods, App. 4
    adhesives, 51, Fig. 4
    banding (or strapping), 51, Fig. 5
    staples and steel stitching, 51, Fig 6
    taping, 51
Coast Guard, 63
Code of Federal Regulations (CFR), Title 49, 57
Commodity codes, 39
Commodity flow survey, 5
Company's characteristics, objectives and performance, 105
Compatability, 83
Competent Authority Approval (CAA), 70
Conditions incident to transportation, 67
Consumer-Consumer (C2C), 31
Consumer protection organizations, 71
Consumer-originating markets, 20
Container (or package) acceptability standards, 47
Container assemblies, 69
Consolidators (see parcel consolidators)
Containers (Type 1, 2, and 3), 45-46
Contract, 97, 98, 103, 104, 114, 116, 117, 119-126
Contract carriage agreements, 120
Contract performance compliance, 120
Contract program, 122
Contracting, 119-126, App. 10
    administration, 126
    competitive bidding method, 122, 123, 124, 125
    evaluation and award, 125
    monitoring, 126
    negotiation method, 122, 123, 125
    sourcing, 123
    screening carriers, 123
    what contracting method, 122
    notification, 124
Control utility, 103
Core carrier program, 124
Core carrier-relationships, 100
Core competency, 5
Corrugated boxes, 76-82, Fig. 15
    folders, 78, Fig. 18
    mailers, 78, Fig. 17
    regular slotted containers (RSCs), 77, Fig. 16
    variable depth boxes, 77
Cost of delivery, 16
Cost of service, 125
Cost recovery, 97, 103
Cost reduction, 103
Cross-border manufacturing, 38
Cubic rule, 101
Cubic size of a parcel, 111, Fig. 23
Cushioning methods
    flotation (also called stuffing), 50
    mold enclosures, 50
    suspension, 50
    wrapping, 50
Customer attention
    high touch, 21
    low touch, 21
    medium touch, 21
Customer requirements, 46, 61, 100, 101, 102, 105
Customer satisfaction survey, 126

D

DC-13 medical device containers, 88
Dangerous goods classes, 63
Data storage capacity, 34
Declared value exception, 101
Delivery date, 93
Delivery Information Acquisition Devices (DIADs), 36
Delivery options, 21, 22
Delivery schedules, 93
Delivery speed, 21
Density of goods, 31
Design qualification tests, 68
Destination address zone, 95
Destination hub, 7
Developments in postal consolidation, 25
DIAD handheld computers, 36
Dimensional weight, 96, 111-112
Disaggregation, 61
Distribution cycle (DC), 88
Distribution of goods, 29
Domestic ground commercial rates, 95, Table 10
Dominant carriers, 9-13, App. 2
Door-to-door service, 102
DOT exemption packaging, 70
DOT label, 65
DOT-E number, 70
DOT-SP-8249 Exemption Packaging System, 70
Double boxing, 49

Drop-ship delivery, 24
Dry ice (or carbon dioxide), 59
Dry ice labels, 59, Fig. 10, Table 6

E
Economical box size, 79
Economies of density, 113
Edge Crust Test (ECT), 80
Electromagnetic or ESD sensitive, 56
Electronic Commerce (e-commerce)(also referred to as electronic marketing), 6, 26-28, 29, 30, 31, 32, Table 5
    advantages, 26
    disadvantages, 26
    e-commerce revolution, 29
Electronic data exchange, 4
Electrostatic discharge (ESD), 86
Electrostatic Protective Area (EPA), 86
Elements (bars and spaces), 33
Elements of packaging
    closure, sealing, and reinforcing, 51
    cushioning, 49
    exterior packaging, 48
    marking and labeling, 55
Emergency exemption, 70
Empty container exception, 65
End user, 28
End-to-end transport, 9
Enhanced DIAD Download (EDD), 36
Enterprise Resource Planning (ERP), 99
ESD Association standard ANSI ESD S8.1-1993– ESD Awareness Symbols, 86
ESD packaging function, 86
ESD protective packaging, 86
ESDS device, 86
Excess value insurance, 101
Expedited service, 102
Expeditors, 25
Export Control Classification Number, 39
Export packaging process, 72, 73
Export packaging standards, 71
Export shipment marking and labeling, 73
Express market, 10
Exterior packaging 48

F
Factors defining parcel delivery
    consumer requirements, 21
    delivery speed, 21
    origin and destination, 20
    shape and weight, 22

FDX Corporation, 11
Federal Aviation Administration (FAA), 63
Federal Express, 8, 10
Federal Hazardous Materials Regulations (HMR), 62
Federal Highway Administration (FHA), 63
Federal Railroad Administration (FRA), 63
FedEx, 10
FedEx Corporation (FedEx), 9, 10, 11
FedEx Operating Units
    FedEx Custom Critical, 11
    FedEx Express, 11
    FedEx Freight, 11
    FedEx Ground, 11
    FedEx Office (formerly Kinko's), 11
    FedEx Services, 11
    FedEx Supply Chain Services, 11
    FedEx Trade Networks, 11
fedex.com, 5, 45
FedEx delivery networks
    air express, 8
    ground, 8
    home delivery, 8
First mile, 25
Fixed network carriers, 8
Flow of funds, 5
Forrester Research, 27
Fourth generation DIAD's (DIAD IV), 36
Freight audit firms, 103
Freight audit issues and concerns, 104
Freight buy, 124
Freight charge, 16, 104, 117
Freight invoice processing, 104
Freight motor carriage
    common, 120
    contract, 120
    private, 120
Freight payment function, 103
Freight payment industry, 103
Fuel surcharge, 97, 109

G
Geographical shipping zones, 24
Global shipping complexities, 39
Global transport, 38
Globalization, 38
Grocery Manufacturers' Association (GMA) pallet, 72
Gross weight limit, 82
Ground and Air Packaging Provisions, 65
Ground delivery, 7, 8, 22

H

Hand-to-surface method, 45
Hazardous material, 62
Hazardous Material Table, 62
Hazardous materials regulations, functional areas
    Packaging Requirements 49 CFR (Parts 173, 178, 179, and 180), 63
    Operations Rules 49 CFR (Parts 171, 173, 174, 175, 176, and 177), 63
    Material Designations 49 CFR (Part 172), 62
    Procedures and Policies 49 CFR (Parts 101, 106, and 107), 62
Hazardous Materials Table, Title 49, Code of Federal Regulations, 64
Hazardous Materials Transportation Act of 1975 (HMTA), 62
Home delivery, 28-32
H-seal (six-strip) versus center seam, 55, Fig. 7
Hub-and-spoke network, 17
Hub-and-spoke terminals, 7
Hub-spoke distribution model, 11
Human body model (HBM) discharge, 86

I

ICC Termination Act of 1995, 120
Insulation
    R-factor, 57
    thermal conductivity or K-factor, 57
    tradition insulation materials, 57
    vacuum insulation panel (VIP), 58, Fig. 9
Integrated airfreight carrier, 40
Integrated carriers, 17, 101
Integrated networks, 8
Integrated transport service, 4
Intermediate hub, 7
Intermodal service (also called multimodal), 4
Internal packaging materials, 50
International Air Transport Association (IATA), 88, 111
International Maritime Dangerous Goods Code of Regulations, 63
International Maritime Organization (IMO), 63
International Organization for Standardization (ISO), 71, 72
International Safe Transit Association (ISTA), 87
International shipments, 96
International trade software
    EasyShip, 41
    Global Trade Manager, 40
    Import Express Online, 41
    InSight, 40
    TradeAbility, 40
    WorldShip, 40
Internet document exchange, 5
Internet-base solutions, 98
Interstate Commerce Commission (ICC), 120
In-transit delivery time, 14
In-transit service variations, 14
In-transit visibility, 17
Irregular shaped items, 22, 112
ISO Standard 6780: Flat Pallets for Intercontinental Materials Handling, 72
ISTA 1 Series Non-Simulation Integrity Performance Tests, 88
ISTA 3 Series General Simulation Performance Tests, 89
ISTA 3A 2004 Test, 89
ISTA Pre-Shipment Test Procedure, 88
ISTA Procedure 1A test protocol requirements, 88
ISTA Procedure 3A, 88
ISTA Procedures and Projects Series, 87

J

Joint-line service, 9
Jupiter Research, 27
Just-in-time (JIT) delivery, 23

L

Labels and placards, 65, Fig. 12
Last-mile, 29
Less-than-truckload (LTL), 9, 20, 23
Linear bar codes, 34
Load, 46
Load types (see package classification)
    easy, 18
    average, 18
    difficult, 18
Local area vehicle, 7
Local distribution centers, 7
Loss, Damage, and Delay Claims
    basic documentation, 117
    basic elements of a claim, 114
    overcharge claim, 117
    responsibilities, 115-117
    suit deadline, 118
    types of damage, 115

M

Machinable, 22
Management Reporting System (MRP), 99
Managing shipping costs, 93
Manual single parcel handling, 18

Marking and labeling, 55, 64, Figures 8 and 11
Markings and symbols, 57
Mass customization, 5
Mass production efficiency, 5
McKee formula, 81
Mechanized sortation systems, 18
Mobile handheld computers, 36
Mobile printer technologies, 35
Monthly-adjusted index-based fuel surcharge, 109
Motor carriage, 120
Mullen (burst) test, 80
Multicarrier shipping service, 98
Multicarrier shipping solutions, 99,
Multimodal (also called intermodal), 3
Multiple orders, 113
Multiple risks, 65

N
National Motor Freight Classification (NMFC), 57, 82, 114
Negotiated rate, 94
Nonproduction shipping, 98
North American (NA) Numbers, 65
Numbered package, 82

O
Obsolete markings, 57
One dimensional (1D) bar code, 33
Order-fulfillment warehouse, 16, 20
Origin address zone, 95
Origin hub, 7
Original manufacturer's packaging, 49
Outsourcing, 105
Oversize charges, 111
Oversize parcels, 111
Oversized shipments (oversize 1, oversize 2 and oversize 3), 112, App. 7, Table 12

P
Package (or container) shipping units (irregular, regular, and smalls), 17
Package Certification Agent (PCA), 69
Package classification, 46
Packaged-product performance, 87
Packaging compliance, 69
Packaging components, 68, 69, 124
Packaging exception, 70
Packaging material specifications, 69
Packaging process, 72-73
Packaging requirements, 63, 105, Table 7
Packaging standards, 72

Packaging system, 59, 70
Packing slip, 55
Padded bags, 49
Pallet (or skids), 75, Fig. 14
Pallet dimensions, 72
Parcel (or small package) delivery, 3
Parcel carrier zone system, 95
Parcel carriers (referred to as integrated carriers), 17
Parcel carriers' pricing strategy, 94
Parcel characteristics, 21, 121
Parcel consolidation, 24 (see shipment consolidaton)
Parcel consolidators, 24, 25
Parcel delivery alternatives
  consolidation and mail services, 100
  drop-shippers, 100
  logistics providers, 100
  regional parcel carriers, 23, 100
Parcel delivery carrier, 7, 8, 34
Parcel delivery industry, 3, 4, 32, 98, 100, 122
Parcel delivery service, 4, 5, 6, 9, 12, 95, 100
Parcel orientation, 19
Parcel Select, 24
Parcel shipping process, 93
Parcel size and weight, 109, Table 11
Parcel volume, 21
Performance Oriented Packaging (POP), 48, 68
Performance oriented tests, 68
Performance packaging, 70
Performance test protocol (D4169), 87
Periodic retest, 68
Perishables, 57
Permeability, 83
Physical transfer, 9
Physical transport, 28
Pictorial Markings for the Handling of Goods, ATSM (D5445), ISO (780), and carrier rules, 57
Pictorial Precautionary Markings (Item 682), 57
Placards, 65
Pooled shipment, 113
Portable Data File (PDF), 34
Postal Rate Commission, 9
Postal Reorganization Act, 12
PowerPad Handheld Computer, 37
Pre-shipment container testing, 87
Pre-shipment test procedures, 87
Pricing strategy, 95, 113
Primary air hubs, 7
Primary rate determinant, 101

Primary risk class, 65
Priority Mail, 13, 14, 31
Private Express Statutes, 13
Product characteristics, 71
Product distribution, 88
Product protection, 72
Product temperature requirement, 61
Production shipping, 98
Profit generation component, 97
Proper shipping name (PSN), 64
Protective function of packaging, 61
Protective packaging objectives, 61
Published (no discount) rates, 94

R
Radio Frequency Identification (RFID), 34, Fig. 3
Refrigerants (coolant), 58-60
Request for Proposals (RFPs)
   automated RFP process, 125
   bid-solutions, 126
   notification, 124
   responsive bids, 125
   solutions, 126
   unresponsive bids, 125
Research and Special Programs Administration (RSPA), 63, 70
Residential (also referred to as noncommercial and private residence), 15, Table 2
Restrictive party screening, 39
Routing guidelines for returns, 94
Rule 222 (for trucks), 80
Rule 41 (for rail), 80

S
Selecting a provider, 106
Selecting a carrier
   parcel delivery alternatives, 100
   critical elements, 101
Service guarantees and refunds, 94
Service levels (also referred to as service offerings, service options, delivery options), 14
Service monitoring function, 108
Service offerings, 3, 14, 95, 100
Services charges, 97
Shape-based pricing, 22
Shape-based submarkets (letters, packets, parcels, and freight), 22
Shipment consolidation, 113
Shipment status information, 32
Shipment (parcel) tracking, 4, 5, 94

Shipper's certification, 119
Shipper's Export Declaration (SED), 39
Shipper's transportation needs, 124
Shipper's transportation profile, 121
Shipping characteristics, 94, 121
Shipping containers
   bags, 85
   barrels, 83
   drums and cans, 83
   sacks, 84
   steel pails, 84
   tubes, 85
Shipping cost, 96
Shipping department, 93
Shipping documents (or records)
   bill of lading, 104, 116, 117, 120
   delivery receipt, 104
   freight bill (or invoice), 104
   weight certificate, 104
Shipping hazards, 18-19
Shipping papers
   hazard class or division, 66
   ID number, 66
   packing group (PG), 67, Table 7
   proper shipping name, 66
Shipping rates, 24, 98, 99, 101
Shipping zone rates, 145, App. 8
Short-term contracts, 119
Shrink-wrap, 74, 96
Single consignment, 113
Single shipment, 120
Single-line service, 9
Six-strip or H-method, 51
Size and weight limits, 109, Table 11
Size-to-weight ratio, 111
Smart labels, 56
Sortation centers, 25
Sorters and sortation systems
   low speed sortation, 37
   medium speed sortation, 37
   high speed sortation, 37
   high speed piece sortation, 38
Special handling considerations, 57
Special Permit (SP), 70
Speed of delivery, 16
Stacking strength, 80
Standard mailboxes, 13
Standard-setting organizations, 71
Static electricity sources, 86
Static shield plastic bags, 86
Stench packaging, 69

Subrisks, 65
Surface Transportation Board (STB), 120

T
Temperature-controlled packaging, 58
Terms and Conditions (T&C's), 45, 109
Third-party logistics (3PL), 104
Third-party payer (3PP), 104
Time-definite delivery, 4, 9, 20
Time-specific delivery, 100
Total shipment weight, 112
Tracking numbers, 102
Traditional delivery process, 29
Traditional store-based commerce, 28, Fig. 1
Transit time, 56, 102
Transport, 4
Transport carriers, 3
Transport charge, 97
Ttransportation agreement, 121
Transportation audit, 121
Transportation costs, 103
Transportation Management System (TMS), 99
Transportation purchasing profile, 121
Transportation spend, 97
Two dimensional (2D) bar code, 33
Two dimensional categories
    matrix symbologies (DataMatrix, MaxiCode, The QR Code), 33-34
    stacked (PDF 417), 34
Two-by-two matrix, 20

U
U. S. Department of Energy, 109
U. S. domestic and international regulations, 63
U. S. Census Bureau's E-Stats Report, 28
U. S. domestic air freight and express industry, 40
U. S. E-Commerce Forecast: 2008-2012, 27
U. S. National Average Diesel Fuel Index
    diesel fuel price, 97
    jet fuel price, 97
U. S. Online Retail Forecast, 2007-2012, 27
U. S. Retail E-commerce, 28
UN and DOT Package Certification Tests
    Cobb Water Absorption Test, 69
    Drop Test, 69, Table 9
    Hydrostatic Pressure Test, 69
    ISTA (Optional) Test, 69
    Stack Test, 69
    Vibration Test, 69
UN and DOT standards, 69
Uniform Freight Classification (UFC), 82

Unit (or unitization), 74
United Nations (Identification) Numbers, 64
United Parcel Service (UPS), 9-10, 24
United States Department of Transportation (DOT), 48, 57, 63, 115, 120
United States Gross Domestic Product, 9
United States Postal Service (USPS), 3, 7, 8, 12-13, 47
Universal Product Code (UPC), 33
UPS Document Exchange, 5
UPS Freight (formerly Overnite), 9
UPS Operating Units
    UPS Capital, 10
    UPS Consulting, 10
    UPS Mail Innovations, 10
    UPS Office (formerly, Mail Boxes Etc.), 10
    UPS Supply Chain Solutions, 10
USPS Board of Governors
    Deputy Postmaster General, 12
    Nine governors, 12
    Postmaster General, 12
USPS Domestic Mail Manual, 47
USPS Facilities
    Auxiliary Sorting Facility (ASF), 12
    Bulk Mail Center (BMC), 12
    Classified Unit, 12
    Contract Postal Unit, 12
    Finance Unit, 12
    Main Post Office, 12
    Post Office Branch, 12
    Post Office Station, 12
    Processing and Distribution Center (P&DC), 12
    Sectional Center Facility (SCF), 12
USPS Products and Services
    Add-on Services, 13
    Airline and Rail Division, 13
    Bulk Mail, 13
    Express Mail, 13
    First Class Mail, 12
    Global Services, 13
    Library Mail, 13
    Media Mail, 13
    Parcel Post, 13
    Priority Mail, 13
    Standard Mail, 13

V
Value-added resellers (VARS), 99
Value-added services, 4, 16, 99, 103
Variable cost characteristic, 8
Variable surcharge, 97

Vendor compliance manual, 90
Vendor packaging compliance, 90
Verbal contract, 119
Volumetric calculations, 111
Volumetric weight, 96

W

Warehouse Management System (WMS), 99
Web-influenced, 28
Weight (actual or volumetric), 111
Wireless technology, 32-37

Workforce characteristics, 8
Written agreement, 119
Written notification, 68

Z

Zone and weight-based pricing, 95, Table 10
Zone numbers, 95
Zone sheet, 102
Zone skipping, 24, 38
Zone table, 95
Zone-based rate, 95

Manufactured by Amazon.ca
Bolton, ON